Online
Teaching
in the
Digital
Age

Online Teaching
in the
Digital Age

Pat Swenson
Nancy A. Taylor
California State University, Northridge

Los Angeles | London | New Delhi
Singapore | Washington DC

Los Angeles | London | New Delhi
Singapore | Washington DC

FOR INFORMATION:

SAGE Publications, Inc.

2455 Teller Road

Thousand Oaks, California 91320

E-mail: order@sagepub.com

SAGE Publications Ltd.

1 Oliver's Yard

55 City Road

London EC1Y 1SP

United Kingdom

SAGE Publications India Pvt. Ltd.

B 1/I 1 Mohan Cooperative Industrial Area

Mathura Road, New Delhi 110 044

India

SAGE Publications Asia-Pacific Pte. Ltd.

33 Pekin Street #02-01

Far East Square

Singapore 048763

Acquisitions Editor: Jerry Westby

Production Editor: Karen Wiley

Copy Editor: Pam Schroeder

Typesetter: C&M Digitals (P) Ltd.

Proofreader: Jenifer Kooiman

Indexer: Sheila Bodell

Cover Designer: Bryan Fishman

Marketing Manager: Jordan Bell

Permissions Editor: Karen Ehrmann

Copyright © 2012 by SAGE Publications, Inc.

Printed in the United States of America

Library of Congress Cataloging-in-Publication Data

Swenson, Pat.

Online teaching in the digital age / Pat Swenson, Nancy A. Taylor.

p. cm.
Includes index.

ISBN 978-1-4129-9619-8 (pbk.)

1. Web-based instruction. 2. Computer-assisted instruction. 3. Distance education. 4. Education, Higher—Computer-assisted instruction. 5. Educational innovations—United States. I. Taylor, Nancy A. II. Title.

LB1044.87.S94 2012
378.1'7344678—dc23   2011031164

SUSTAINABLE FORESTRY INITIATIVE

Certified Chain of Custody
Promoting Sustainable Forestry
www.sfiprogram.org
SFI-01268

SFI label applies to text stock

This book is printed on acid-free paper.

12 13 14 15 16 10 9 8 7 6 5 4 3 2 1

Contents

Acknowledgments

We wish to acknowledge several colleagues at California State University, Northridge (CSUN). These individuals have been proponents of online teaching, and we are very grateful to them for their support over the years: Pamela Bourgeois, Cathy Cheal, Donald E. Hall, John Hartzog, Kara L. Klima, Barbara Kroll, Patricia Y. Murray, Robert Noreen, Kimon Rethis, Ilene Rubinstein, Cheryl Spector, Sandra Stanley, Sheryl Thompson, and George Uba.

To our two editors and reviewers—Michelle Hutchens (professional technical writer and owner of http://www.procom.us/) and Dr. Terrie Mathis (Professor of Linguistics and English at CSUN)—we couldn't have done this without you.

We would like to thank our families and our friends for their support and understanding.

A very special thank you to our dear friends Dennis and Allen for their unconditional love and support. Finally, to P.Y., our lifelong source of inspiration and our spiritual foundation, we offer you our unceasing love and gratitude.

Preface

You've been assigned an online course but may have limited knowledge of the educational technologies prevalent in today's virtual Web 2.0 world. Your new appointment conjures up many uncertainties from your days as a new teacher (or perhaps you are new to teaching now), and struggling against panic, you wonder how you will survive this experience. A flurry of thoughts and questions about learning and implementing new technology, time management, and student needs bombard your mind . . .

- How can I teach an online course if I have no knowledge of webpage creation?
- If I've never participated in an online chat room or forum, how will I manage an online discussion?
- Will my institution provide technical support, or am I expected to learn about online teaching independently?
- How will I manage the time to confidently learn new Internet applications?
- Will my traditional course materials easily and effectively transfer online?
- How do the expectations of online students differ from those of traditional students?
- How can I ensure active student participation?
- Will I be inundated by student email regarding technical issues?

What Our Book Can Do for You

Throughout the book, we address practical aspects of online teaching by referencing our decades of combined experience. Chapter 1 explores and defines the learning theory that serves as a basis for our online teaching philosophy. Chapter 2 delves into the inner workings of Learning Management Systems (LMSs). Chapter 3 examines the innovative mainstream educational applications currently available on the Internet. In Chapter 4, we offer our personal examples and guidance in creating and maintaining an efficacious virtual learning environment. In our final chapter, we provide helpful suggestions and have included a semester-end checklist to assist with your introspection process. Lastly, our appendices provide samples of online syllabi, schedules, and virtual classroom etiquette.

For knowledgeable online educators, we've included a section on incorporating streaming audio and video as well as popular features such as *Facebook, Google Docs, Blogger, Ustream,* and *YouTube.* Experienced instructors may prefer to read specific sections pertinent to their own situations. If you're new to online instruction, you may prefer to read each section of the book sequentially. Whatever your level of expertise, we have arranged our book in a way that will enable you to quickly and easily find the answers to your questions.

Using simple lay terms, we will instruct you in the basic knowledge you need to successfully teach an online course. You will learn how to take the materials you use in your traditional classroom and transfer them to your new virtual environment. You will learn, with confidence, how to run real-time (synchronous) and time-arranged (asynchronous) online discussions. Perhaps, most reassuring of all, you will learn that very few of your traditional course elements need to change.

The good news (and there's a lot of good news) is that, no matter your choice in application, the material provided in our book will assist you in designing and implementing effective online courses for years to come. To assist you in proactively cultivating technical proficiency in the virtual classroom, we highly recommend recording your weekly course activities in a personal journal throughout the semester. Highlighting your interactions and experiences will assist you in objectively evaluating your performance. Vital to your success as an online educator, you will need to be able to determine which applications effectively serve your needs.

As with the more traditional classroom instruction you're accustomed to, you will discover, through trial and error, apparatuses and approaches that work effectively with an online student audience. Your first course design won't be your last. You will continually tweak your approach and style to fit the changing needs of online learners. But for now, fear not. Help is on the way! You can do it!

1

The Virtual Classroom

A Dynamic Learning Environment

Overview

The rapidly changing nature of technology has had a striking impact on students' modes of expression. The online environment emphasizes empowerment through the written word, and our new group of online learners has grown up in the Web 2.0 world of texting, blogging, and tweeting. Today's students often utilize several social networking sites to interact with their peers, and as they participate in such activities, they consistently frame their ideas and opinions in writing. Due to the pervasive impact and popularity of such sites, today's youth may interact more easily with computers than they do in face-to-face contexts.

In this chapter, we provide the theoretical framework that shapes and defines our teaching philosophy as it relates to online instruction, and we will discuss how implementing that ideology translates into creating and building an effective online classroom. When we first started teaching, Social Constructivist Theory framed our methodologies, and interactive learning and teaching served as the core of our classroom ideology. Our experience has shown us that the most productive learning environments tend to be the ones where the student and teacher co-create the educational experience. Paulo Freire refers to this as *co-intentional* education, whereby both student and teacher become equalized in the pursuit of knowledge.[1] Such an

---

[1]Freire, Paulo. (1997). *Pedagogy of the Oppressed*. New York: The Continuum Publishing Company, 51.

egalitarian concept serves a highly useful purpose in online education as students learn more when they are equal participants. As you will read in this chapter, creating a dynamic, interactive environment functions as the core of a successful online classroom.

Social Constructivist Theory and the Online Learning Environment

Social Constructivist Theory provides, unintentionally or intentionally, the foundation of the Learning Management System (LMS). As discussed in more detail in Chapter 2, an LMS is a software application that your educational institution has licensed, enabling courses to be taught online. The founders of the disparate LMSs developed their systems with the idea that student and teacher co-develop the dialogue of the class. Social Constructivist Theory focuses on learners as "active constructors rather than passive recipients of knowledge."[2]

Our institution, California State University, Northridge (CSUN), currently uses the open source software Moodle for its online courses. Moodle (originally an acronym for Modular Object-Oriented Dynamic Learning Environment) follows the Social Constructionist pedagogy in its very design. The Moodle community (along with many other LMSs) supports co-intentional education and Constructivist Theory as its components create a platform that encourages all participants to share the roles of teacher and learner. Through use of interactive discussion, teachers move from being "the source of knowledge" to being an "influencer, role model, and moderator," and students begin to engage in a "deeper reflection and re-examination of their existing beliefs."[3]

Within such a proactive environment, the teacher no longer functions as the sole authority figure. Successful LMSs capitalize on this idea by making the student the focus of the learning environment. By emphasizing the interactive nature of online teaching, the use of an effective LMS helps maintain a high level of enthusiasm for learning. For those of you who already implement Social Constructivist Theory in your classrooms, you will gravitate easily to the learning structure provided by the LMS; for those who teach primarily lecture-based courses, this may prove to be a revolutionary

---

[2]Lewis, Barbara A., & MacEntee, Virginia M. (2005). Learning Management Systems Comparison. *Proceedings of the 2005 Informing Science and IT Education Joint Conference.* Retrieved January 15, 2011, from http://www.informingscience.org/proceedings/InSITE2005/P03f55Lewis.pdf

[3]Philosophy. (2009). *Moodle.* Retrieved September 17, 2010, from http://docs.moodle.org/en/philosophy

shift from the teacher-oriented to the student-oriented classroom. Whichever category you fall into, you will discover that Social Constructivism creates an effective base for the virtual classroom.

By having Social Constructivism serve as their foundation, LMS creators provide a variety of synchronous (live, real-time) and asynchronous (time-arranged) platforms upon which instructors can develop their classes to appeal to the broad spectrum of the population that encompasses today's learners. Based on our experience, today's online learners function better in environments where they have some level of responsibility for their own educations.

Re-imagining Classroom Roles: Today's Online Learners

Online education assists us in re-imagining traditional classroom roles in non-traditional classroom settings. Web-based discussion establishes a mutual interchange in which the student is both participant and audience, demonstrating Paulo Freire's theory of co-intentional education, where all persons in the classroom (teacher and students) share the task of unveiling, critically analyzing, and re-creating knowledge.[4] Incorporating learning technologies such as small group and whole-class forums or blogs and live chats can foster such student interaction and ingenuity.

When you require participation, you create a student-centered pedagogy in your online classroom and vastly improve the depth of your discourse. By applying Paulo Freire's theory of empowerment to encourage students to feel like masters of their own thinking, you will

- equalize all voices;
- empower and motivate students;
- promote student-to-student interaction (and collaboration);
- create a community of writers;
- provide a larger audience base, resulting in a heightened focus on clarity, substance, preciseness, literacy, and critical thinking; and
- increase exposure to a multitude of voices and points of view.

Following these guidelines, you challenge students to re-think stereotypical and simplistic viewpoints. By encouraging counter-opinions, students begin to analyze their own thinking processes. The result is a deeper relationship with the material at hand as students are more likely to utilize their learned knowledge once they are no longer in the classroom.

---

[4]Freire, Paulo. (1997). *Pedagogy of the Oppressed.* New York: The Continuum Publishing Company, 51.

Screen Capture 1.1 A look inside Blackboard's LMS interface: the instructor notifications dashboard.

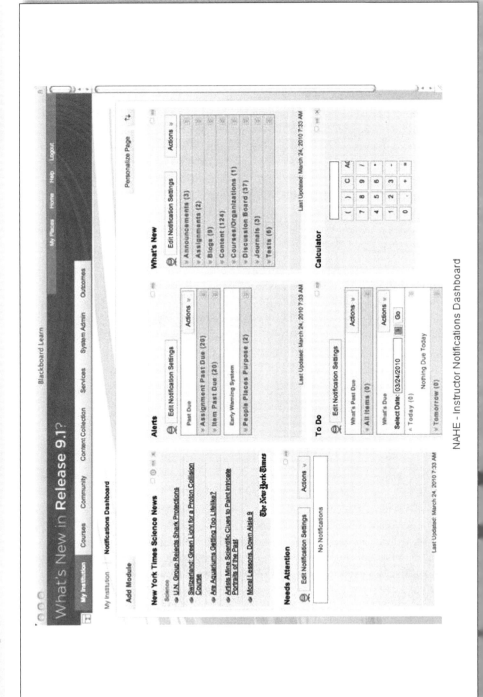

NAHE - Instructor Notifications Dashboard

Scholars have noted the sagacious dialogue present among students during online discussions. In their comparative study of Learning Management Systems, Lewis and MacEntee stress the social nature of online learning, and in keeping with contemporary constructivist theory, they recommend the use of dynamic and interactive online course components to meet the needs and expectations of today's active social learners. Course content with a student-centered approach (including a variety of discussion modules) will allow participants to play active roles in their own learning experiences.[5] In their analysis, Lewis and MacEntee also point out key differences between traditional and online students:

> Students who take on-line courses tend to be self-directed learners. They show initiative, independence, and persistence in learning. As they accept responsibility for their learning, they see problems as challenges rather than obstacles. They share a high degree of curiosity, a strong desire to learn, and the capacity for self-discipline. They can set goals, make plans, organize their time, and set an appropriate pace for learning.[6]

With regard to the type of student who signs up for online courses, we need to note an additional observation. As we teach at a state university, budgetary constraints dictate course offerings. At our university, several types of students, therefore, sign up for online courses. Most will be self-motivated, while others may enroll in an online course because their school's funding cuts may have reduced the offering of traditional courses. Be aware of a potential diverse group of online learners registering for your online course; economics may force less "self-directed" learners into your virtual classroom.

Your Role as Online Instructor

As an instructor in an online classroom, your role is multi-faceted; of course, your primary concern is to teach your subject matter. However, how you construct your course activities is of equal importance. Once again, a key concept to keep in mind (one that defines the online environment of the LMS) is the social nature of learning. Lewis and MacEntee maintain the necessity of choosing the right course components—student-centered

---

[5]Lewis, Barbara A., & MacEntee, Virginia M. (2005). Learning Management Systems Comparison. *Proceedings of the 2005 Informing Science and IT Education Joint Conference.* Retrieved January 15, 2011, from http://www.informingscience.org/proceedings/InSITE2005/P03f55Lewis.pdf

[6]Ibid.

content such as forums and chat discussions that emphasizes active, reflective, and social learning.[7] In creating a comfortable setting, students will thrive in environments where they serve as active participants in the pursuit of knowledge.

Student-to-student interaction constitutes one of the core concepts of the efficacious virtual environment; consequently, you'll want to incorporate a variety of discussion formats into your classroom, allowing the students to connect with the material and one another on deeper and more meaningful intellectual levels. Although technology offers varied modes of discussion that can seem sterile compared to in-person dialogue, some of these platforms actually provide deeper means of connecting between students and teacher, resulting in a greater authenticity of written and spoken communication. If you can find a way to integrate synchronous and asynchronous course elements, then you'll find you can more readily guide and monitor student interaction with the material, and the students will more effectively grasp and connect with the topics discussed.

In *Empowering Education: Critical Teaching for Social Change,* Ira Shor espouses the value of student empowerment:

> Participation is the most important place to begin because student involvement is low in traditional classrooms and because action is essential to gain knowledge and develop intelligence. . . . People begin life as motivated learners, not as passive beings. . . . But year by year their dynamic learning erodes in passive classrooms. . . . Their curiosity and social instincts decline, until many become nonparticipants. . . . Participatory classes respect and rescue the curiosity of students.[8]

Active use of technology, whether in an asynchronous or synchronous classroom, elevates the atmosphere to one where the motivated learner thrives, contributing to more fruitful dialogue among students and between the students and teacher. In constructing meaningful dialogue with your students, you allow participants a greater voice and a greater willingness to have their voices heard. Embrace Ira Shor's philosophy of open participation, and your students will find themselves more inclined to dialogue with you and with the course material.

---

[7] Ibid.

[8] Shor, Ira. (1992). *Empowering Education: Critical Thinking for Social Change.* Chicago: The University of Chicago Press, 17–18.

Summary

When you first approach your online classroom, establish an atmosphere where open dialogue thrives, and you will create a successful learning environment. Have your students serve as co-creators in the construction of your virtual classroom, and you will find that they will retain the course material more effectively. Remember—your role is to guide your students, to demonstrate to them that they have active roles in their own learning processes. By creating a student-centered curriculum, you will find that your fear will lessen and your online classroom will become defined by dynamic cooperation.

Due to the popularity of the Web 2.0 social networking sites, most students already engage in active communication and will be receptive to trends in Social Constructivist Theory and co-intentional learning. The current LMS design inherently supports today's active social learning environment and facilitates success in the virtual classroom. Encourage active participation, and your online community of self-directed learners will flourish.

2

Establishing Your Web Presence

The Learning Management System and Course Webpages

Overview

In an online course, all activities and correspondence will be handled over the Internet through a variety of available tools, such as a Learning Management System (LMS), webpage design, discussion forums, blogs, chat, and email. Your institution will most likely have a license with an LMS freeware or commercial provider, and the Internet provides access to a variety of free mainstream educational resources. In setting up your course, you will need to choose an online platform; you have three primary options, which you may use independently or in conjunction with one another. You may

1. Use an LMS.

2. Establish a web presence by creating course webpages using HTML or xHTML/CSS.

3. Choose open-source mainstream Web 2.0 Internet applications.

In this chapter, we will give you the nuts and bolts to the first two approaches (the final approach, Web 2.0, will be addressed in detail in Chapter 3). You may choose a blended approach, as we have for our courses (see Chapter 4); however, your choices may be dictated by whether your class meets synchronously (live) or asynchronously (time arranged) and whether your class is entirely virtual or hybrid (partly online).

Since there are many commercial and freeware LMS options, we will provide you with a general overview of the common features of most LMS software available to instructors. Please check with your institution for information on its specific LMS. If you elect the LMS option, please note that all content is private and secure, available for viewing only by students enrolled in the course. By solely choosing this option, you will not create a web presence; therefore, your efforts cannot be found by ways of an Internet or campus-wide search (look for more on the benefits of creating a web presence later in this chapter). For now, we will present an overview on the LMS tools available to you. When you have finished reading this chapter, you will have an understanding of the kinds of support and applications an LMS provides online educators.

Learning Management Systems

What is a Learning Management System? An LMS, also commonly referred to as a Course Management System (CMS) or a Virtual Learning Environment (VLE), is a software application your educational institution has licensed enabling courses to be taught online. Although there are over 100 viable LMS software programs available, most offer a similar range of helpful features for online teaching. Whether commercial (such as Blackboard or Joomla) or open-source freeware (such as Moodle and Sakai), your institution will choose a range of training and features to help you to create, manage, and upload your course content online.

For our purposes herein, we will provide an overall analysis of LMSs. Your institution will choose among the many commercial and freeware options, and in many cases, your academic technology division will supplement the LMS with additional programming or software. What we have provided below is a general overview of what the majority of LMS software programs offer. We strongly recommend that you view your institution's online tutorials, read applicable software documentation, and if possible, attend in-person training workshops to better familiarize yourself with the specific options of the LMS at your institution.

Turning Your Traditional Course
Into an Online Course

Every tool you will need to teach an effective and dynamic online course is available on the LMS. You will have a variety of collaboration tools and activities to choose from, most notably live chat, discussion forums, quizzes, and audio/video upload. Your administrators may program your open-source or commercial LMS to include a wide variety of options, so collaboration tools will vary. Our university, for instance, has chosen to integrate the anti-plagiarism program Turnitin into our LMS; it has also acquired a license for the live web-conferencing program Elluminate. All added features are most likely embedded within the LMS for easy access and navigation.

Your LMS may have a calendar feature that enables you to organize and display your course schedule week to week, and you can choose to upload course content into this weekly calendar format for easy and orderly access. LMS course controls within the calendar are usually integrated with a student view option, so you can toggle between your editing and how your work will be viewed by your students. You may have the option to keep the course, or selected elements of your course, hidden from student view until you have uploaded all of your instructional materials.

LMSs provide you with the ability to upload documents and to create links to external websites in the course content area (with or without the calendar feature) for viewing by students. For lectures, you have several display options:

- Upload document files directly into the LMS and then display the files as links.
- Length permitting, copy and paste your material directly onto the course content page.
- Copy and paste your lecture into a discussion forum.
- Record and upload your lectures as MP3 or MPEG files.

If PowerPoint is your preferred software application, you may need to host your presentation on another website (check with your IT department regarding your LMS's capability to host PowerPoint). You may also save your PowerPoint as a video file (see PowerPoint's help section for more information) and then follow your LMS's directions for uploading a video file. Please note that PowerPoint is not compliant with the Americans with Disabilities Act (ADA); additional software is needed for accessibility conversion of PowerPoint graphics.

If you intend to incorporate professional multimedia from the Internet into your course, you have the option to embed popular external video players such as YouTube, QuickTime, and RealPlayer. Each LMS should provide instructions for uploading audio and video files and for embedding video players into your course content pages. It's often as easy as adding a link!

Regardless of which features you choose to incorporate into your course, most LMSs will allow you to upload an unlimited amount of content. Most will provide a file management system for you to create folders and organize your uploaded files as well as an option to back up your course content. Most LMS software enables you to copy previous course components, so

Screen Capture 2.1 Moodle course page with calendar feature displayed.

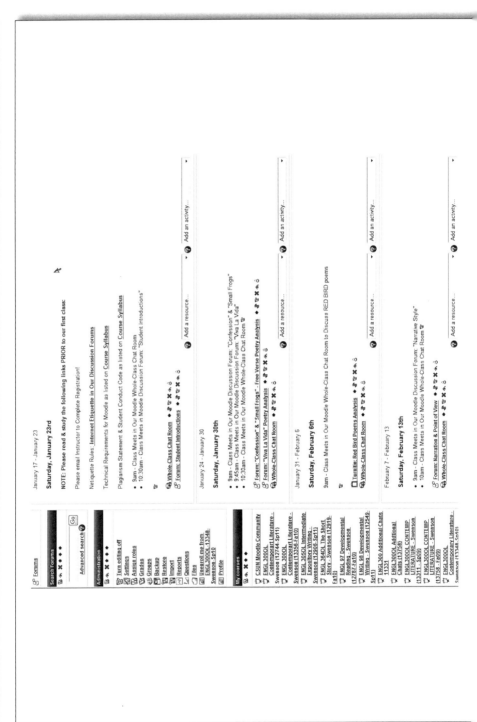

once you create your course template, you will have the ability to transfer all course items to a new course. As with traditional classes, subsequent semesters become much easier.

Managing and Monitoring Your Students

Enrollment

Many institutions link enrollment and course registration directly into their LMSs. Once you create your course page, students will be automatically enrolled onto your LMS roster. Students who add your course after the start of the semester should appear on your LMS roster within 24 to 48 hours. Please note that a student who drops your course may have to manually un-enroll from the LMS. To ensure that late adds have access to your course, you can either provide a temporary access key code or disable privacy permissions so guests may enter. After the add deadline, simply switch the permissions back so only enrolled students can view your course page.

Messaging Students

Communication between students and faculty within the LMS is accessible and viable. To email a private message, click on a student's profile. Some LMSs keep a copy of the message in the student's profile; others only send your message via email. Our Moodle system has a default whole-class news forum for course announcements. This news forum acts as a class email LISTSERV; when posting in this discussion forum, we have the option to send our message as an email to the entire class. Some LMSs may provide a message history area for you to view all of your correspondences with the entire class or with an individual student.

Forum Setup Options

Depending on the flexibility of your LMS, you will have partial or complete control over the parameters of your discussion forums. You may

- Limit student accessibility.
- Limit the number of posts.
- Hide student posts (alter visibility).
- Select a threaded (outline-style) or unthreaded format.
- Require students to subscribe to a forum (each post would then generate an email).

- Control the amount of time students can post (establish open and close dates).
- Determine aggregation (point allotment based on quantity of posts).
- Upload files and images.
- Track unread messages.
- Select groups manually or engage the automatic (alphabetic or random) sorting feature for group forums.

Real-Time Chat Features

When creating a chat activity, you can allow all students to participate, or you can restrict student access by selecting the group feature (very handy for small-group discussion). As with forums, you can choose group members, or you can let the LMS automatically sort students into groups. You may have an unlimited number of chat rooms active at one time, and you will be able to monitor and participate in the rooms simultaneously as long as you select yourself as a member of each group. Most live chat features offer you the choice to log and save transcripts for future reference and student review; you may make these transcripts public or keep them private. Some chat rooms have private messaging enabled; if so, we suggest you disable this feature so your students focus only on the live chat discussion! Some LMS software programs, such as Blackboard, and the web conferencing program Elluminate, for example, have an additional whiteboard/blackboard feature for illustrating course elements during live chat. Many have sound notification; you can choose to be notified by a beep when a student enters or exits the chat room.

The Quiz Module

The quiz feature in many LMSs offers a variety of question types, and most software enables the instructor to mix and match multiple choice, true or false, short answer, matching, and essay questions in one exam. Some quiz software also permits you to vary the point allotment within a quiz, so you can assign a higher or lower point value to certain types of questions. With the exception of the essay portion, the quiz feature automatically calculates a student's grade and, subsequently, records it in the grade book. You may create your questions from scratch or import them from your own computer, which is a very practical feature for those wanting to incorporate quizzes from their traditional courses. Once uploaded, the LMS automatically creates a quiz bank, and your questions will be stored for future use. Some LMSs allow students multiple attempts at answering a question or taking an entire quiz. To discourage academic dishonesty, some quiz features allow

Screen Capture 2.2   Moodle whole-class discussion forum.

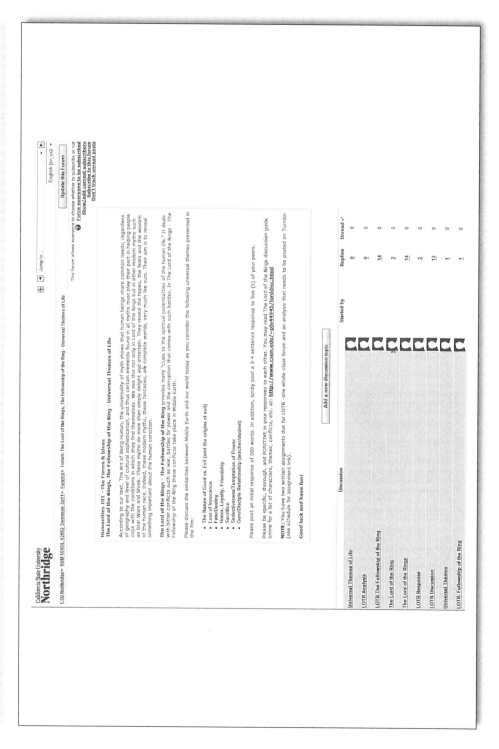

California State University
Northridge

⊞ ▼ | Jump to... ▼

English (en_us) ▼

Humanities 101 – The Forms & Ideas
The Lord of the Rings, The Fellowship of the Ring - Universal Themes of Life

According to our text, The Art of Being Human, the universality of myth shows that human beings share common needs, regardless of geography and level of cultural sophistication, and thus certain elements found in all myths must play their part in helping people cope with the conditions in which they find themselves. We see this not only in Lord of the Rings but in other modern myths such as Star Wars and Shrek. These myths do more than simply delight and entertain. They reveal the hopes, the fears and the wisdom of the human race. Indeed, these modern myths, these fantasies, are complete worlds, very much like ours. Their aim is to reveal something important about the human condition.

The Lord of the Rings - The Fellowship of the Ring provides many "clues to the spiritual potentialities of the human life." It deals with bitter conflicts such as war, battles for power and the corruption that comes with such battles. In The Lord of the Rings - The Fellowship of the Ring these conflicts take place in Middle Earth.

Please discuss the similarities between Middle Earth and our world today as you consider the following universal themes presented in this film:

- The Nature of Good vs. Evil (and the origins of evil)
- Loss of Innocence
- Fate/Destiny
- Honor, Loyalty, Friendship
- Sacrifice
- Seductiveness/Temptation of Power
- Guru/Disciple Relationship (teacher/student)

Please post an initial response of 500 words. In addition, kindly post a 3-4 sentence response to five (5) of your peers.

Please be specific, thorough, and POSITIVE in your responses to each other. You may read The Lord of the Rings discussion guide online for a list of characters, themes, conflicts, etc. at: **http://www.csun.edu/~pjs44945/lorddisc.html**

NOTE: You have two written assignments due for LOTR - one whole-class forum and an analysis that needs to be posted on Turnitin (see schedule for assignment link).

Good luck and have fun!

This forum allows everyone to choose whether to subscribe or not
❶ Force everyone to be subscribed
Show/edit current subscribers
Subscribe to this forum
Don't track unread posts

Update this Forum

Discussion	Started by	Replies	Unread ✓
Universal Themes of Life		0	0
LOTR Analysis		0	0
LOTR: The Fellowship of the Ring		14	0
The Lord of the Ring		2	0
The Lord of the Rings		14	0
LOTR Response		2	0
LOTR Discussion		13	0
Universal Themes		1	0
LOTR: Fellowship of the Ring		1	0

Add a new discussion topic

15

Screen Capture 2.3 Elluminate live chat discussion with whiteboard feature.

you to randomize the order of the questions and answers and set specific or limited dates and times to take the exam. A variety of quiz and grade reports can be generated by the instructor; charts can cross-reference how many students answered a question correctly.

Student Assessment

Your LMS provides many ways to view and assess student activity; merely by clicking on a student's name, you may be able to see at a glance the complete course history for each student, including

- the total number of posts, views, and hits to your discussion forums;
- date and time of first and last log-in;
- total time spent online;
- time spent in forums; and
- time spent on other course content.

Most software contains a log feature that enables you to view class activities at a glance. Live logs, statistics, activities, grades, and participation reports for all or individual participants are available with a click of the mouse. You will be able to monitor and track the activity levels and participation of each student, including how often a student logs into your course, views, and responds to your course material.

Grading features in your LMS may include instructor assessment, student self-assessment, peer assessment, group feedback, automatic and manual scoring, and a grade book which you can customize to include certain categories and percentages, points, aggregation, and so on. Your program may be able to generate a grader (instructor) and a user (student) report.

In your settings and preferences, you may choose an aggregation strategy to establish the means and modes of grading for your course. Most grade book software automatically calculates and registers grades, and these grades may be made visible or hidden from view. When creating quizzes and discussion forums, you may choose point values; both can be automatically assessed and recorded into your grade book. Please note the subjectivity of discussion forum grading. Forums can be set up to automatically calculate a grade by quantity, not quality, of posts. You may also choose to manually assign forum grades, and if this is preferable, display the grades to avoid student email inquiries. If your LMS has an anti-plagiarism program such as Turnitin embedded into its software, you can also select a point value or percentage for each student essay. Once you manually assign a grade to a student paper, the grade book feature will record it.

Establishing a Web Presence:
Creating Course Webpages

If you choose not to use a CMS or to use it minimally, you will need to create a website for your course syllabus, schedule, assignments, lectures, and discussion links. Check with your institution's technology department for pre-designed single-column or multiple-column templates for home pages, syllabi, schedules, biographies, and assignments. If you create your own webpages, choose clarity and accessibility over style. Explain in detail your contact information, course requirements, meeting times, and locations, and provide links to your discussion forums, chat rooms, quizzes, and multimedia. Since there will be little or no face-to-face communication, make sure everything is clearly stated on multiple pages. You may also need to make your web content widely accessible, meeting the standards of the ADA. Contact the IT web developers on your campus for your institution's accessibility policy and for federal and state compliance guidelines (see section 508 of the Rehabilitation Act of 1973 at www.section508.gov). Website validation tools are available online to scan webpages for ADA compliance and are easily found by means of an Internet search.

As we previously mentioned, we use a blended approach for our online classes and have established a web presence by creating course webpages that are accessible to all who surf the Internet. Remember that your LMS course page is not public; it is viewable only to enrolled students. By providing our information to the entire web, we engage in content sharing between students and faculty on our own campus and elsewhere. By establishing a web presence, we become searchable entities in our university's search engine and on the Internet en masse. Keep in mind that, when students are contemplating which courses to add, they can view your content if it is made public on the Internet. Your web presence can increase enrollment in your courses and attract new students to your institution. An additional benefit—making course information public results in fewer email inquiries.

Because we teach in the state of California, our university IT division has authored ADA-compliant file templates and has licensed Adobe syllabus-building software products such as Contribute, Dreamweaver, and WYSIWYG (What You See Is What You Get) to enable faculty to create and edit webpages without having to write HTML or xHTML/CSS code. Our university requires all instructors to upload their syllabi onto the web to be made available to the public; you may also be required by your state or institution to maintain a web presence. Check your institution's IT website for specific requirements.

Screen Capture 2.4   Sample HTML syllabus webpage.

Many universities provide software downloads and ready-made templates that have consistent and coordinated design schemes, making it quite manageable for faculty to type in their specific details and then upload their course webpages onto their school's servers. Little knowledge of writing HTML code is necessary; however, more advanced users will be able to adjust the code and design if they desire to do so. As LMS course design remains static, learning to write your own course code will provide you with more control and flexibility over your course design, most notably banners and image displays. Your institution likely provides in-person workshops on webpage creation, online video tutorials, or written documentation. Once you feel comfortable with the online environment and are ready to take on a more advanced web presence, we highly recommend that you learn how to create your own course webpages. To assist you, we have provided sample syllabi and schedules in our appendices.

Summary

Whether you are teaching a synchronous or asynchronous course, carefully consider the online resources provided to you by your learning institution. For newcomers, we strongly suggest the security of an LMS. LMSs provide a one-stop shop for educators; these commercial and freeware applications come equipped with calendar features and file management systems to assist you in uploading and maintaining your course material, a variety of discussion modules, a quiz maker program, assessment options for online grading and monitoring student activity, and a means for embedding multimedia onto your course pages.

When considering your choice of platforms, please keep in mind that maintaining a web presence ensures content sharing between students and faculty on your own campus and elsewhere and can increase enrollment in your courses and attract new students to your institution. Little knowledge of HTML code is necessary; many universities provide software downloads and ready-made templates that have consistent and coordinated design schemes, making it quite manageable for faculty to edit and upload to their course webpages. Before you finalize your decision, you'll want to consider the Web 2.0 alternatives we present in the next chapter.

3

Web 2.0

A World Wide Web of Options

Overview

We are living in a new, interactive, and collaborative Web 2.0 world with many mainstream Internet technologies and applications available for use in the virtual classroom. If your online teaching career necessitates a journey beyond the Learning Management System (LMS), you may find yourself venturing into the ever-growing and ever-changing market of open-source learning. User-generated applications and social networking sites such as Facebook, Google Docs and Blogger, YouTube, Skype, and Ustream provide an innovative foundation for online curricula.

With education budgets on the decline, there is a general tightening of expenditures; subsequently, sources such as Google Educator have risen in popularity, especially in the venue of public education. Given today's economics, you may have to rely on the cost-free Web 2.0 applications currently available on the Internet. Even if you have an LMS at your disposal, you may find yourself feeling adventurous at some point and wish to explore these popular alternatives.

As you implement mainstream applications, keep at the forefront both privacy and Americans with Disabilities Act (ADA) accessibility concerns. Some tools and applications may have more lenient privacy standards than an LMS, so take extra precautions in maintaining the integrity of written work. As the popularity of mainstream education sites increases, software developers are striving to provide content that is universally accessible. State

Screen Capture 3.1   Google Educator main page.

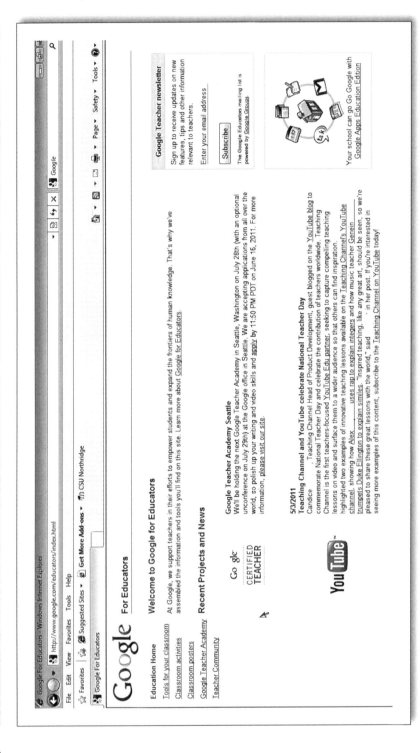

and government compliancy law is often more stringent for academics, so contact your IT department to determine if your choice of mainstream applications meets the minimum compliancy standards of the ADA.

Web 2.0: Mainstream Applications

If you find using an LMS's discussion and teaching modules too inflexible for your needs, or if you simply want or need to expand beyond your educational institution's licensed programs, you may consider supplementing your online course with the following web-based applications currently available on the Internet. Internet giant Google has developed Google Educator, which incorporates Google Docs, Blogger, and a variety of other applications designed for classroom use. Facebook, the leader in social networking, features tools for blogging, messaging, real-time chat, and media sharing. YouTube and Ustream can provide for your streaming audio, video, and lecture needs, and Skype is effective for live conferencing and virtual office hours. Table 3.1 illustrates the educational features available on these popular mainstream sources.

Although primary sources of the new Web 2.0 can supplant more traditional LMS features, none of the aforementioned educational tools support anti-plagiarism detection software. While there are mainstream options for checking originality, most require a paid subscription. Google Alert offers a free, albeit limited, detection service by way of the Google search engine. If your institution has a license with an anti-plagiarism program such as Turnitin, consider using mainstream Web 2.0 learning and teaching tools in tandem with the resources provided by your institution's LMS.

Social Networking: Facebook

Facebook provides the most popular avenue to connect with students on their level of communication, and this free mainstream application offers a variety of innovative applications appropriate to the virtual classroom. Most notably, Facebook serves as a web host for discussion blogs, streaming audio and video, live chat, and instant messaging. Within Facebook, you can create groups; disseminate information; share pertinent quotes, links, photos, and multimedia; and relate to your students on a more personal level.

Most commercial websites offer options to share articles and videos on Facebook, affording educators a valuable tool in incorporating current events and media into the online platform; you can also add links to an

Table 3.1 Educational Features Checklist.

Application	Educational Features								
	Messaging/ Notification or Email	Word Processing	Peer Editing	Whole-Class Live Chat	Discussion Blog	Small Group/ Individual Conferencing	Virtual Office Hours	Media Sharing	Streaming Audio/ Video for Lectures
Facebook	✓	✓	✓	✓	✓	✓	✓	✓	
Google Docs	✓	✓	✓		✓				
Google Blogger	✓				✓			✓	
YouTube								✓	✓
Ustream								✓	✓
Skype						✓	✓		

unlimited amount of video hosted from sites such as YouTube. Having used Facebook in our online courses, we have a few suggestions for implementing it into your online curriculum.

Although Facebook functions primarily as a social networking site, it also offers academic-enhancing possibilities, the most valuable aspect for educators being the newly designed group page. Facebook recently added new beneficial rules for setting up group pages: Members now have the option of setting up a group page that is closed (open only to invitees) or open to any account holder (anyone can join). If you choose to have a group page for each of your courses, then select the closed-group option and invite participants accordingly. You may also consider creating one group page for all of your students; should you select this option, you will need to widen your topics to include a more general educational or social tone.

As group administrator, you select how much freedom you want to offer your members. You can restrict posts to the group wall, you can be the sole provider of information and then permit your students to respond to the topics or media you share, or you can choose an open submission policy and allow students to post their own opinions and material. An advantage of using Facebook over the tools offered by the university is that Facebook makes it easier for the students to add content.

You will have numerous ways to display course information as each group page provides the following categories for sharing on the wall: Post, Link, Photo, Video, Event, Doc, and Poll Question. Facebook formats each type of post, so once a category is selected, a dialogue box pops up to assist you in posting. It's remarkably intuitive, fun, and easy! An instructor can disseminate information or engage students in discussion by posting quotes, questions, timely news videos, images (personal or from around the Internet), music videos, and links to external webpages.

Facebook can serve as a mainstream learning tool for forum discussion (blogging), live group chat, and email LISTSERV. The group wall is quite similar to a forum discussion; the main difference is seen in the format and storage of posts. A typical LMS forum offers a more organized and accessible way to view all threads in a discussion; a blog or a Facebook discussion may get buried in a long list of discussion threads. While still accessible, a participant may have to scroll quite a way down the page to access an older discussion. To counter this, you could use the Facebook Docs feature as a way to conduct a discussion. Docs can be uploaded and edited by all members, and they will display on a separate Docs page separate from the main group wall. Your Doc could pose a discussion question, and group members would select *edit* to add to the bottom of the document.

In tandem with wall discussion features, Facebook also supports live chat with an unlimited number of participants. On the bottom of the group

Facebook page, students may click the chat box icon, which will substantially enlarge the chat screen. Students may need to be instructed to enable the live group chat function in Facebook.

In addition to chat, Facebook offers a private messaging feature that can substitute for a class email LISTSERV. Each group administrator has the option to message individuals or the entire group; students will receive messages in their personal Facebook in-boxes, and as long as the email notification feature for messaging is selected, they will be notified via email whenever a message is sent out.

If you elect to incorporate Facebook into your online classroom, we offer the following suggestions to protect your and your students' privacy:

- Create a new email account for Facebook. Since you will receive notifications and possibly email messages from members, we advise you to keep this separate from your personal or campus email. It's very easy to create a Yahoo, Hotmail, Google, or AOL email account—and you will be grateful that you did.
- Instruct your students not to add anyone to the group. There is a feature/link to invite new members. Either disable it or dissuade your students from adding people who are not on your roster.
- To ensure your own personal privacy, we suggest that you refrain from adding your students as your "friends." If you do decide to add students as friends, they will be able to access your personal Facebook page and see all of your posts, pictures, and information, and they will also be able to post on your wall. There are numerous privacy settings available, but once you befriend someone, you will need to block undesirable "friends" on an individual basis. It's simpler to keep students on the group page and avoid inviting them to be your friends. Our advice? Do not open this Pandora's box!

As administrator, you are at the controls. Please remember to check with your IT department for your institution's rules on ADA accessibility. Please note that Facebook makes frequent changes to its interface.

Google Docs

Google offers a free web-based word processing application known as Google Docs. Once you sign up for a free Google email account, you can access this real-time collaboration tool and begin to edit your documents online from any computer. Users can create new text documents, spreadsheets, presentations, drawings, and forms, and most file formats (including Microsoft Word, PowerPoint, and PDF) can be uploaded directly into the program.

There are several options for visibility and ownership, and Google Docs has a pull-down menu feature to select what works best for each of your documents.

The owner of the document can assign permissions to share and edit to an unlimited number of participants. Depending on your choice of assignment, you can share a document with an entire class or limit accessibility to small groups or individual students. You can allow all students to edit or select just a few. For individual paper assignments, students can upload their documents onto your Google Docs course page; you can then choose who views and edits each document. For group workshops or presentations, students can upload to your page, or you can require them to create their own pages and then subsequently give you viewing and editing privileges for their course documents.

Because Google Docs lends itself naturally to collaboration, you may wish to choose this mainstream platform to conduct writing workshops that require peer review. Documents can be edited in real time, so if your course meets live, your students can simultaneously comment on student papers or projects. The program also offers a notification option; if selected, then participants with editing privileges will receive email notification when there are changes to a document. Please be advised that, at this time, Google Docs has not integrated a tool for anti-plagiarism. If you are concerned about originality, you can copy and paste in a few key phrases from your student papers into Google Alerts (http://www.google.com/alerts).

Additional Mainstream Options

Blogs

Conduct an Internet search for blog-creation sites, and you will come up with a variety of options for creating your own blog. On the very top of your search results, you might find Blogger, a free blog hosted by Google. Many free and commercial blogs provide design templates and video tutorials, most offer to host your blog on their website, some allow you to upload photos and video, and most should provide similar privacy options for sharing and posting. If you choose to use a mainstream blog in lieu of an LMS discussion forum, you will need to designate a significant amount of time to set up your page and permissions. If time management is an issue (especially for those new to online teaching), consider relying on the ready-made LMS forums for your blogging needs. Once you have reached a comfort level in teaching a variety of online applications, you may find freedom in a mainstream blog.

YouTube

If you are interested in incorporating mainstream media, YouTube is a popular and very reliable hosting source. Like Facebook and Google, there is no charge for an account or access. You can sign up for an account and upload video onto the YouTube website then simply ask your students to visit your YouTube page, or you can embed the YouTube video player (simply via the embed link YouTube provides) into your LMS, Facebook, or Google page. Our university has its own YouTube page; we are free to sign up for an account in order to store our videos all in one place. Although the Fair Use Act should enable you to upload a portion of commercial video for educational purposes, always check for copyright permissions.

Streaming Audio and Video

If you are interested in producing and broadcasting your own lectures, you can purchase your own software and hardware and create streaming audio and video lecture presentations. Inexpensive computer software is available for you to record your own voice at home using a microphone. This software enables you to save your audio in a variety of formats that are compatible to your LMS or Web 2.0 application. Your computer's webcam can be used to broadcast a live lecture and discussion. You can also audiotape or videotape a traditional classroom lecture you've given to use in a subsequent online class. These audios and videos can then be saved and uploaded for future viewing.

A few popular mainstream webcasting sites exist for streaming audio and video. At our university, we are fortunate to have Elluminate, a web-conferencing application, embedded into our LMS. Many mainstream applications, such as Facebook, Google Docs, and Blogger, have media-sharing capabilities; once you save your own lectures as media files, you can upload them onto the aforementioned websites. Our university has also established a video production service that provides educators with a recording studio and necessary software to format streaming video to the QuickTime format. We highly recommend that you contact your IT department for available in-person or online options for recording and streaming live and recorded audio or video.

Ustream

For those without an LMS or an on-campus video recording option, you may wish to create an account with Ustream, a website that offers a platform for live broadcasts and streaming video. With your computer webcam or a video camera, you can broadcast live or stream your recorded lectures to a wide audience. You can upload your videos onto Ustream's website, or you can download a video player and broadcast live from your own channel. If

Screen Capture 3.2 Elluminate's web conferencing feature.

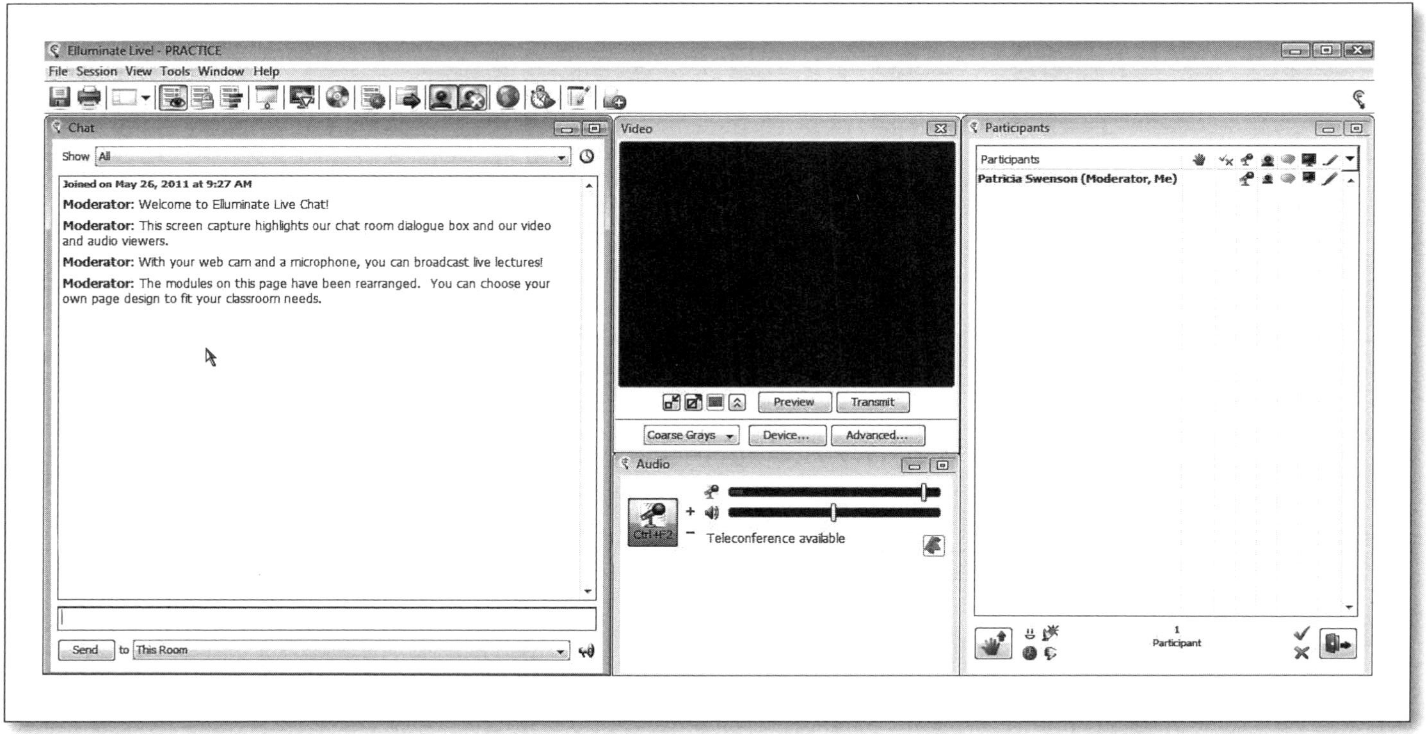

you choose the video player option for your live lectures, your students will also need to download the player onto their own computers and then link to your account. The basic streaming video feature is free, but cost will vary if you desire a professional-quality broadcast and storage system for your taped lectures. For lectures on the go, you can even record yourself on an iPhone and upload it to Ustream!

Skype

The group video and conference software Skype provides a more limited mainstream option for live streaming video. If you choose to Skype, then all participants must subscribe (it's free) and upload the software and player onto their personal computers. A broadband connection and webcam are required. Prior to conferencing, all contacts (participants) must join and link to your account. To participate with a group of 10 (the maximum number of participants per session), you will need to sign up for the premium service or request a video subscription from the Skype Manager. There is a minimal monthly fee or pay-as-you-go option for these premium services.

Perhaps the best and most efficient use of Skype would be for a virtual office hour or one-on-one discussion. Because the maximum number of participants cannot exceed 10, live whole-class discussion is highly improbable. For students who may be overseas, or if you are traveling during the semester, Skype provides a free means for private communication.

Please remember, as with all mainstream applications, you will need to check with your institution regarding accessibility of blogs, chat, and video. The ADA, as applied in your area, may have more stringent rules regarding education, so if you intend to use mainstream commercial applications in your classroom, be sure to check with your IT department for state and federal accessibility requirements.

Summary

For more experienced online educators, those feeling particularly adventurous, or those teaching virtual classes on a tight budget, Web 2.0 offers enticing, fun, and free options such as Facebook, Google Docs and Blogger, YouTube, and Ustream. These commercial sites offer components comparable to what is found on the LMS platform, and most provide an array of tutorials and group help forums to assist you in your initial setup. From blogs to chat to streaming multimedia, the mainstream Internet contains a variety of options for disseminating your course information. As an added benefit, you'll find that students gravitate toward these popular interactive technologies.

As you set up your course, you'll find a range of diverse options for many of your technological and educational needs. Whether you choose a mainstream or academic platform for your courses or a combination, inquire as to your institution's requirements for accessibility and ADA compliancy. As mainstream websites advance in popularity as free alternative options for educators, most are making strides in privacy and accessibility for all learners. We hope you enjoy the vast array of Web 2.0 tools available to you.

Links to Mainstream Websites

Many commercial sites offer free resources, tutorials, and discussion blogs for educators who wish to incorporate a portion of their curricula online. The links below provide you with a wealth of information:

Elluminate: http://www.elluminate.com/

Facebook: http://www.facebook.com/

Google Educator: http://www.google.com/educators/index.html

Google Blogger: http://www.google.com/educators/p_blogger.html

Google Docs: http://www.google.com/educators/p_docs.html

Google Alerts: http://www.google.com/alerts

QuickTime: http://www.apple.com/quicktime/

Skype: http://www.skype.com/intl/en-us/home

Twitter: http://twitter.com/

Ustream: http://www.ustream.tv/

YouTube: http://www.youtube.com/

4

Choosing Your Course
Format and Features

Overview

In the first three chapters, we discussed online learning theory, the nuts and bolts of a Learning Management System (LMS), and a variety of mainstream teaching tools found on the Internet. In this chapter, we integrate our personal experiences as evidence of the efficacy of the aforementioned topics. Our combined decades of online teaching experience provide a practical, proven guide to constructing an effective and sustainable online course.

The coming pages highlight strategies for the initial setup of your course as well as ways to create, grade, assess, and moderate student forums and live chat. Your first objective is to determine how you will display and disseminate your course information. For those new to online teaching, we suggest you rely on the LMS licensed to your institution. Here, you will find all the collaborative and instructional tools you will need to successfully teach a virtual course. Early in your online teaching career, we recommend that you create a web presence by uploading your syllabus and schedule onto your institution's server. Your webpages will provide public access to your course materials and will serve as a necessary backup in case your LMS goes offline.

In addition to prominent discussion features, we recommend adding a variety of learning modules, including a quiz maker and a platform for reviewing essays, to effectively instruct and assess the diverse population of online learners. Discussion forums may provide the foundation for your asynchronous classroom, but should you have an opportunity to teach a live online course, we strongly suggest implementing a combination of real-time chat and forum discussion into your curriculum. These two discussion platforms complement each other; you will discover that whole-class discussion forums strengthen small and whole-class chat sessions. Having students submit responses to your discussion forum topics before synchronous interactions effectuates a richer conversation during the chat sessions. Lastly, for those concerned with time management issues, we offer suggestions for training and familiarizing yourself with features and collaboration tools. In this way, you will be better prepared to create a course template that can be utilized in future semesters.

Approaches to Displaying Course Information

As mentioned in Chapters 2 and 3, you need to determine how you will display your course information, including your syllabus, schedule, assignments, important links, and contact information. Because we have been teaching online for the past decade, we have always maintained a web presence by uploading our HTML course documents onto our university's server. In the early days of online teaching before the advent of the LMS, faculty needed to learn HTML code (and later, with compliancy laws, the Americans with Disabilities Act (ADA)–accessible xHTML/CSS code). All course information found its home on webpages, and additional links had to be provided for external chat and forum applications. In today's Web 2.0 world, however, the majority, if not all, of the beginning online instructor's needs can be met by using an LMS.

We choose to utilize a blended approach to ensure we have a backup system in place in case our LMS goes offline or is down for maintenance and to ensure our web presence. Please remember that if you solely use an LMS, you will not establish a web presence on the Internet; therefore, we highly recommend adding a webpage containing at least a syllabus to ensure that students can access your course information at all times. Content sharing and course accessibility are key benefits to all online learners and educators. We strongly encourage you to look at the design of the available educator webpages so that you can see what appeals to you.

For those of you who do not currently design your own pages or do not have ready-made templates available from your institution, the one-stop shopping approach of an LMS is designed with you in mind. Using an LMS during your first year of online teaching will dramatically decrease your anxiety levels and help with time management demands. Once you achieve a solid understanding of LMS components and how they function in the online classroom, you may then choose to begin attending workshops or view online tutorials on webpage creation.

Display Options

Whether you choose to use a webpage or an LMS, you will have a variety of tools available when you decide how to display your course content. If you choose to design your main course page within your LMS, you will have the following display options:

- Type in text that will appear on your main course page.
- Upload course documents such as syllabi, schedules, assignments, and lectures. When uploading documents, the most efficient program to utilize would be Microsoft Word or a similar mainstream word processing program (see your LMS help feature for document format compatibility).
- Create forums that house vital information, such as course requirements, assignments, and so on.
- Disseminate messages via email or a course LISTSERV. If sent via the LMS, then your LMS will store a copy of your correspondence, which will be accessible to students for future review.
- Provide links to external websites, including course information stored on your institution's server.

Using Simple Text to Create a Syllabus and Schedule

One basic option for displaying course information is to simply type your syllabus and schedule directly onto your main LMS course page. You can type all weeks in one area or use the calendar feature to separate and isolate each week. If your course meets live, choose the dates listed on your university's schedule for your course meetings; if your course is time arranged, choose which days you wish to begin and end each week. Our asynchronous online courses begin on Sunday and end on Saturday, with posting deadlines at midnight each Saturday night. Consistency is clarity; inconsistency is insanity—choose the same due date each week!

Most LMS programs allow you to choose how to display your main page. If you type in your entire course requirements, you will discover that you have created a rather lengthy main page. Students will need to scroll down to see your entire course content, thus increasing the likelihood that vital information or important links will be misread or even missed. Therefore, if you choose to include all of your information in one place, we strongly encourage you to place any important links, including links to chat rooms, discussion forums, and assignments, at the top of your page for easy viewing. An additional option for increased clarity—use the *visibility/ invisibility* command on your weekly calendar feature to hide the weeks that have been completed.

Screen Capture 4.1   Sample LMS course webpage with text.

California State University
Northridge

You are logged in as **Patricia Swenson** (Logout)
English (en_us) ▾

CSU Northridge▸ ENGL3000L

CSUN

CSUN Home Page
Oviatt Library Resources
IT Help Center
Academic Technology
Student Moodle Help

People
🖉 👁 ✖ ✦
👥 Participants

Activities
🖉 👁 ✖ ✦ ✦
💬 Chats
📝 Forums

Search Forums
🖉 👁 ✖ ✦ ✦

[   ] Go
Advanced search ❓

Administration
🖉 👁 ✖ ✦ ✦
📝 Turn editing off
🗒 Settings

❓ Switch role to...

Topic outline

Welcome to Pat Swenson's English 300 OL!

Greetings! We will be using Moodle for our weekly whole-class threaded discussions and LIVE chats! Please read our schedule carefully for all due dates and assignment links.

Please click this link to **Our English 300 OL Syllabus** and follow all course guidelines.

Live Chat & Weekly Threaded Discussions

You will be required to discuss course material with your fellow students in our Moodle threaded discussions and chat rooms. All topics, requirements and due dates are listed in each threaded discussion and on our schedule page. NOTE: Please visit our page on Turnitin to post ALL of your Major Paper Assignments (see schedule)!!!

Please practice courteous behavior and respect each other's viewpoints!

Please read our Internet Discussion Etiquette Guidelines prior to our first chat.

To confirm your enrollment, send me an email prior to our first class.

Best of luck to you!

♻
📝 News forum ✦ 📋 ✖ 👁 ✦ ♻

❓ Add a resource...   ▾   ❓ Add an activity...   ▾

Turn editing off

Latest news
🖉 👁 ✖ ✦ ✦
Add a new topic
(No news has been posted yet)

Upcoming Events
🖉 👁 ✖ ✦ ✦
There are no upcoming events
Go to calendar
New Event

Recent activity
🖉 👁 ✖ ✦ ✦
Activity since Tuesday, May 24, 2011, 10:26 AM
Full report of recent activity...

Course updates:

Deleted Forum

Blocks
🖉 👁 ✖ ✦ ✦
Add...   ▾

Uploading Documents

In lieu of manually typing your information directly onto your main page, you can upload your course documents directly into the LMS. These uploaded documents will appear as links; once they have been clicked on, your students' computers will open up the appropriate word processing program. (Note: Mac users may have to convert documents into a Word, PDF, or TXT format. Check your LMS's document format compatibility.)

With access to documents, your students can view your syllabus, schedule, assignments, and lectures online, or they can download them onto their own computers, and if they would prefer paper copies, they have access to printer-friendly versions. Choosing this format shortens the display of your main LMS page: Your course page will then most likely display only a series of important links and images and multimedia players, should you choose to include them. If you already have your course work saved as Word or text documents, then this may be your easiest and least time-consuming choice as you can simply upload the documents you have created for your traditional classes.

Using Forums to Display Course Content

You also have the choice of creating and designating forums to display a variety of course content, such as syllabi, schedules, lectures, and assignments. The forum editor gives you the choice of using an HTML editor or using simple text. You can place the forum links on your main course page; the LMS also automatically stores all of your forums (once you make them visible to students) in one place on a separate page for easy reference. When you create a forum, most LMSs offer the option to email either a notification or the actual forum content to all students on your roster. You may also choose to disable responses to forums that house your course syllabus and schedule if you do not want students posting questions and comments. The forums you create can be imported to your next semester's LMS course page, and the LMS will automatically delete the previous student responses so you can begin with a clean slate. This option significantly reduces your time demands during subsequent semesters.

Dissemination Via Email

You may disseminate your course information via email or, more specifically, a course LISTSERV. The LMS will give you an option to email all members on your roster and will store your information in a forum for easy reference. For example, our IT department has programmed a default news forum in Moodle for instructors and students to post general course information. When authoring a new message, you have the option of selecting *mail now* to send your forum post via email to all participants. Your message will also permanently display on a sidebar on the main page until you choose to delete it. What is the primary advantage of sending an email through the LMS? When your students reply to the email the LMS generates, their responses are sent only to you and not the entire class.

Your institution may also automatically generate an email LISTSERV independent from the LMS. This LISTSERV will contain the school email addresses for all students currently registered in your course. Please note that you will always have some students who do not use their campus email; therefore, they may miss your initial LISTSERV messages. Students will need to take responsibility (after some gentle prodding) to either check their campus email or forward their campus email to their preferred email client. If you rely on a course LISTSERV, please understand that your students may respond to a class-wide message with a personal or minor matter, thus clogging up both your and your students' inboxes. Our campus only gives permission to the instructor to send messages via the LISTSERV, so when a student hits *reply*, the system generates an error message to all members. Because of the aforementioned potential problems, we prefer to communicate through the LMS messaging system. Check with your IT department for specific guidelines regarding your LISTSERV permissions.

A course LISTSERV works most effectively when used to send notifications of messages or changes that need to reach students quickly. With one email, you can communicate to your entire class; however, by solely relying on email, you will not establish a permanent place to store all of your course information. Vital announcements and requirements won't be readily accessible to you or your students. We suggest using the LMS LISTSERV because it chronologically stores all messages for future reference. If you do not use an LMS, then consider storing course information on your webpages, as you will want to have an accessible storage and display system for important messages and changes to course information.

Links to Course Websites Outside the Learning Management System

Prior to the advent of the LMS, we established a web presence on our university's website and, subsequently, the entire Internet. To this day, we create and store the bulk of our course information on university webpages external to our LMS. Our university offers ready-made, ADA compliant templates for a syllabus and schedule, and with our knowledge of HTML and xHTML code (learned over a period of time by attending numerous campus workshops and by reading commercially available books and articles on web creation), we have adjusted the templates to fit our design and course needs.

We maintain a general main page that lists our contact information, department information, and links to the current courses we are teaching. This is the URL we provide to the public, and students can then click on the appropriate course to view the syllabus, schedules, assignments, lectures, links to the LMS, and other media and Web 2.0 resources (see our appendices for sample syllabi).

Our online course material does not vary significantly from the documents we produce for our traditional courses: We incorporate standard course requirements, grading breakdowns, instructor contact information, university regulations, and compliancy and accessibility statements. In addition to the common elements found on most traditional syllabi, we've added a section on technical requirements, links to any necessary software add-ons and downloads (such as recent additions of Java, Adobe Reader, and Flash), online course components, our campus tutorials, and our IT Helpdesk.

As we have noted, course webpages provide a partial backup to the LMS as basic information such as your syllabus, schedules, lectures, and assignments can be publicly accessed via the Internet. Our university currently uses the freeware software Moodle, and since it is freeware, it isn't supported by a major software developer. We have experienced some occasions when the system has been overloaded and rendered inaccessible to both faculty and students. More specifically, our chat system often crashes if too many students are online at one time. Several times a semester, IT may perform maintenance, also resulting in intermittent outages. These potential issues serve as an added impetus for creating your own webpages external to the LMS. It would indeed be rare for your LMS, university website, and email LISTSERV to simultaneously go offline, so integrating all three into your course serves as a considerable fail-safe. Whichever path you choose, please consider an easily accessible and reliable backup plan for disseminating your course information.

The Virtual Classroom: Choosing Your Course Features and Learning Tools

When you are assigned an online course, you may be able to choose to teach the course asynchronously (time arranged) or synchronously

Screen Capture 4.2   Sample main HTML webpage with contact information.

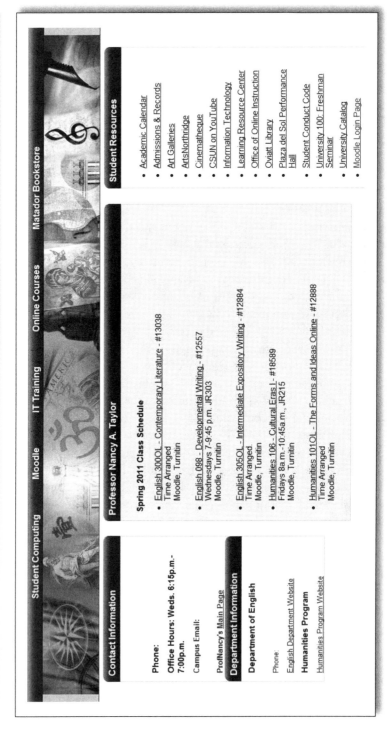

(live, in real time). Synchronous courses meet live online every week, and you determine the specific course tools; the university establishes a set course meeting time. Your schedule outlines when and where to meet, with fixed times for live chat, forum discussion, quizzes, and exams. Asynchronous courses are time arranged, with no live meeting time or place. Work needs to be completed weekly, bi-weekly, or bi-monthly, for example, based on the deadlines created by the instructor. We have included an example of both synchronous and asynchronous course schedules in our appendices.

Depending on your teaching style, the most substantial time demand may involve the initial setup of your first online course. You will need to decide how to make your course content interactive and engaging, and you will need to choose features and collaboration tools to incorporate into your main LMS page. Your course template may include learning activity modules, such as discussion forums, live chat, quizzes, databases, lectures, and multimedia. Most universities offer workshops or provide online written documentation or tutorials on specific LMS elements, so do take advantage of those. If your university does not offer workshops, peruse the Internet for online help forums that may contain beneficial information or guidelines. Our LMS system, Moodle, has its own Moodle Community, an online help desk within the LMS that is moderated and maintained by campus IT facilitators.

The Asynchronous Classroom: Forums, Essays, and Quizzes

Discussion Forums

When it comes to setting up your asynchronous online course, you'll find that one of the most important elements involves the creation and implementation of whole-class discussion forums. As forums provide ways for students to interact with the material and one another, you will come to rely on whole-class forums as the principal mode of discussion in your time-arranged online classroom.

To construct effective discussion forums, you will want to scaffold your assignments. When we compose the initial forum question(s), we require an initial response of 250 to 500 words. The second part of the forum assignment asks the students to return to the forum, read through the postings of their peers, and reply to several of their peers' posts. Students may engage in a lengthy back-and-forth dialogue regarding a given post, but we suggest instructing students to make sure everyone receives at least one response to his or her initial analysis. We recommend requiring the students to reply to at least three and upwards to five (or more) of their peers, depending on the size of enrollment. As you set guidelines for the replies, consider asking the students to compose at least three to four thoughtful and detailed sentences that incorporate the ideas presented in the original post. We also suggest that you make your posting timelines clear and consistent. As an example, for asynchronous classes, you might require the students to post their first response by Thursday (this assumes that you have your week begin on Sunday and end on Saturday). If you give students until Saturday to post their first responses, those last-minute postings won't reap the benefits of feedback from their classmates as a consequence. Another meaningful point to consider regarding posting deadlines—if all students wait until the very last minute to post their initial responses, there will be no time available for reading and responding to peers. Moreover, the original posts of students who post late may not receive peer responses. Setting firm deadlines helps increase the interactivity among students, and you will see that your forums will serve as a more effective collaborative educational tool if you provide sufficient time for peer-to-peer interaction. (For suggestions on using forums in a synchronous course, see the section in this chapter on "Synchronicity: The Real-Time Virtual Classroom.")

An excellent way to introduce students to the forum process involves having them become acquainted with each other in the beginning of a semester with an "introductory, getting-to-know-you forum." A student introduction forum helps ease all participants into the online process as they will be given the chance to familiarize themselves both with the class and with their peers. This initial relaxed discussion also provides them with an opportunity to practice online posting. We make the introductory questions lighthearted and informational. We also ask students to post their email addresses, a necessary step in helping to sustain and build a dynamic online community. Exchanging email addresses builds a database of people to correspond with should there be questions about the course; furthermore, asking students to solve their own problems student-to-student enables them to collectively take responsibility for their own work.

If your goal is student empowerment, then we recommend that you avoid adding your own voice to the forums. We have learned that forums work more effectively when we maintain their teacher-free integrity. When the instructor posts in the forums, it alters the dynamic between the students and may cause them to feel less responsibility while framing their own peer responses. Whole-class forums serve to maximize exposure to a variety of student points of view as well as maximizing participation, and as we

Screen Capture 4.3 Student introduction discussion forum in Moodle.

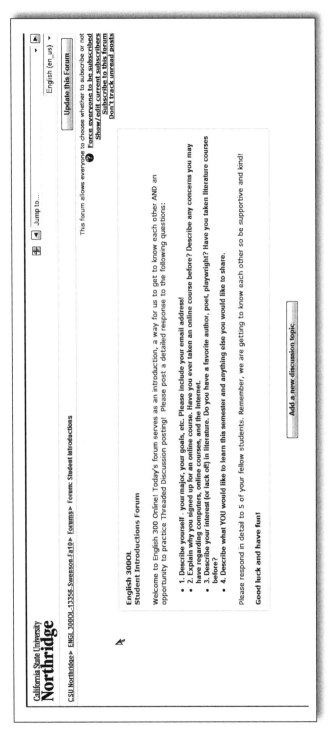

pointed out in Chapter 1, this creates an empowered and dynamic online classroom environment.

Here are a few important guidelines to follow when setting up whole-class forum discussions:

1. Set a time by which the first posting must be completed.

2. Set a time by which the students must respond to one another.

3. Set guidelines for what students need to accomplish when responding to one another's posts, such as length and number of posts, encouraging an ongoing dialogue, preserving an open-mindedness and respect for all opinions and points of view.

4. Instruct the students to compose their responses in word processing programs and to save their work. If they compose their writing within the LMS and the LMS goes offline before they click *submit* or *post,* they will lose their work. This is a frustrating experience, and oftentimes, students may use this as an excuse for late or missing work.

5. As you post your writing prompt, include any necessary links to additional information, external websites, images, or videos.

6. Determine grading aggregation and select manual (grading on quality) or automatic (grading on quantity). Indicate to the students within your writing prompt the point value of each forum.

7. Choose to keep the forum open for late posts, or select a close date.

8. Post the link and the title of your discussion forum in several places for easy accessibility. Place the link in your schedule, in your calendar, and on top of your main LMS course page. Visibility and clarity are key!

Forum Assessment

Once you're ready to set up your whole-class forums, you'll need to start thinking about how you will assess student performance. Will you set up assessment based on quantity or quality of work? We'll provide you with some disparate assessment methods, so you'll be able to choose which works best with your teaching style, time demands, and subject matter.

LMSs offer the option of grading forum responses based on the quantity and timeliness of student posts. This style of grading is completely objective; students earn points based on the number of posts and the time of posting. At the close of the deadline, the LMS automatically registers a grade (or a point total based on how you set up the forum parameters) to the students' profile pages. In courses with high enrollment or multiple forum assignments, automatic grading based on quantity reduces your time commitment to the course; however, you need not assess all of your forums in this manner. You may reduce grading time by designating some forums to be graded on quantity and some on quality. If you choose a combination of formats, make your grading guidelines clear to the students by stating within the forum question itself how student work will be assessed. Remember, if you choose to assess your students' work based on quality, you'll have to manually enter their grades into the grade book feature.

When we grade discussion forums for our courses, we read the posts individually and assign grades based on content and effort. This takes more time but also serves as a thorough assessment of the students' interaction with, and understanding of, the course material. It also affords us the opportunity to become better acquainted with our students and their writing styles, and since forums do not have anti-plagiarism systems, to determine the originality of the work posted.

Because of the give-and-take nature of forum discussion, you will need to determine how much weight the students' original responses earn versus their responses to their peers. We make the original post worth at least 50 percent, with the remaining percentage calculated based on responses to peers. Choosing a manual grading method such as this does not allow for the use of the LMS automatic grading system; therefore, the assessment process may take a considerably longer amount of time.

Essays, Peer Review, and Assessment

If you assign written essays and would rather avoid having students post them in public whole-class forums, you have several options for privacy, some of which will require longer setup and assessment time. For these longer essay assignments, you may

1. Create individual private forums for each student.

2. Create a quiz, featuring an essay-only requirement.

3. Require students to email their work in a Word document.

4. Require your students to upload their papers onto an anti-plagiarism application such as Turnitin if your institution has a license.

Before our university attained a license for Turnitin, we either created individual forums to house each student's work or required students to submit their individual papers via email. To check for originality, we would copy and paste any suspicious line or section of text into a search engine (see section on "Google Alerts" in Chapter 3). This is a more time-consuming option for investigating potential academic dishonesty but one well worth considering if you do not have access to an anti-plagiarism program.

A program such as Turnitin has a helpful feature called GradeMark, which contains pre-set comments that you can integrate into an essay you are evaluating. Pre-set comments include how to fix comma splices, run-ons, awkward phrases, and a variety of other common grammatical and punctuation issues. GradeMark also provides the option to create your own pre-set comments, and it saves these comments from semester to semester so you don't have to continually recreate them. If you do not have access to a feature such as GradeMark, or you are responding to student writing in a forum or via email, you can create your own list of common comments, save in a document, and pull from the list each semester. As you comment on essays, simply copy and paste from your list.

For classes that incorporate writing workshops or collaborative projects, Turnitin offers a PeerMark feature that enables you to set up small-group review within the program. The general GradeMark comments are available for student use in PeerMark. Again, if this is not a viable option, you may conduct peer review in your LMS by creating several small-group forums. To facilitate the workshop or collaborative process, you may wish to provide your students with your own list of common comments.

Quizzes and Exams

We have found that incorporating quizzes and exams into the online classroom provides inventive variety to the learning experience, especially for courses that require a great deal of memorization and reading comprehension. Quizzes, as long as they do not include essays, can be automatically graded, thereby saving you a significant amount of time. If you choose to create longer essay exams by using your quiz maker feature, you will need to manually evaluate and grade the essay sections. As an additional benefit of quizzes and exams, your LMS system publishes the results into each student profile. Once you've created a quiz or longer exam within your LMS, it will transfer over if you wish to use it in subsequent semesters.

Synchronicity: The Real-Time Virtual Classroom

If you choose to conduct your course synchronously, you will be in for a lively and invigorating experience! Real-time chat can be an enjoyable feature because the live format provides you with an opportunity to bond with your

Screen Capture 4.4 Turnitin.com website.

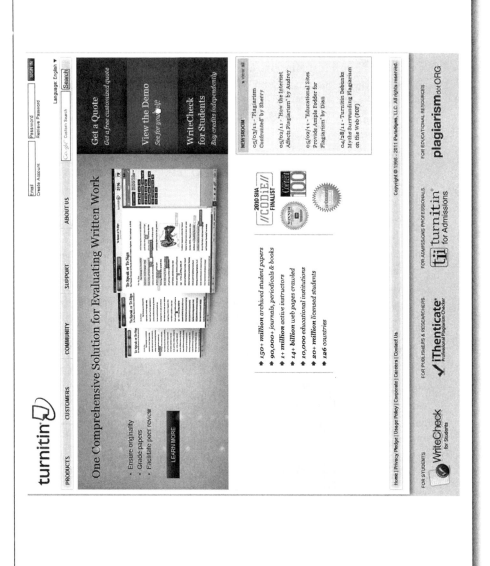

47

students. You may even have the chance to "see" their faces (as they will yours) if your LMS allows participants to upload images and avatars. You will have the opportunity to "hear" their voices, and in turn, they get to "hear" yours.

Moderating a Chat Session

Conducting a live chat session takes patience and a solid system. By providing an online handout on chat etiquette (see more about Internet etiquette in our appendices), you will be establishing a how-to-behave-online contract between you and your students. Students will understand the rules for participation, and they will understand that they must respect others. Creating guidelines for chat and disseminating them prior to the first class meeting will help you to maintain an orderly and prosperous live discussion.

When instructors choose to utilize real-time chat in their online curriculum, some common questions arise:

- What happens if I encounter technical difficulties? What do I do if the chat malfunctions and students get logged off?
- My students are so experienced chatting online, and I've never stepped foot inside a chat room. How will I be able to control and conduct a chat session?
- How do I sustain an in-depth and productive class discussion (one that engages and involves the majority of students) over the entire designated chat time?
- How do I deal with inactive, absent, or rude participants?

Except for the technical difficulties, you would respond to these questions as if you were conducting an in-person traditional class. Most chat systems record participants: when and how often a student logs on and off and how many times a student participates. If a technical glitch occurs and the system goes down, simply encourage all participants ahead of time to find their way back into the chat room. The LMS re-records the names of those who re-enter the chat room. If the system remains down for several minutes, you may need to send an email with further instructions to your class LISTSERV. If chat goes down but the rest of the LMS is working, you can send your students back into a discussion forum to engage in a thoughtful dialogue by posting additional responses to peers. It's the rare occasion when you will be forced to cancel the remainder of a class due to a lengthy system failure, but it can occur.

The LMS essentially takes roll for you each time a student logs on. However, it is important for students to realize that there is a distinction between logging on and participating in a chat. We recommend taking roll based on participation; merely noting that someone has logged on does not ensure that they actually have a chat room presence. The most effective way to ensure that students partake of and read the chat is to require that they participate. Students who remain idle for long periods of time may not be paying attention to the discussion. They may not even be in front of their computers! That's why we have a chat participation rule on our syllabus:

> In order to earn credit for participating in a chat, each student must make at least ___ quality thoughtful comment(s) per discussion. Fulfilling this mandatory requirement illustrates that you are satisfactorily interacting with the material.

By clearly mandating active participation and succinctly stating this policy on your syllabus, you encourage students to take responsibility for their own educations, and equally as important, you empower them through this required exchange of ideas. When you mandate participation, you maximize participation. Expect many students to "raise their hands" voluntarily (an exclamation point for a comment, a question mark for a question—for more etiquette rules, please see our appendices). Since the chat screen can scroll quickly when there is a lot of participation, we suggest that you keep a pad and pen handy, so you can write down the names of the students and call on them in the order in which they raise their hands. Although this allows for an orderly and structured method to conducting the course discussion, occasionally you will, as we have, miss a student's name as the conversations can at times go by at a rapid pace. This is normal, and your student may bring it to your attention. Simply apologize, and place them next on the list.

If you notice that a particular student has not been participating, feel free to call on that student. Despite the fact that many students feel safer and more secure speaking through a computer keyboard, some students are painfully shy and reticent. For these types of students, we suggest that you have a list of simple questions nearby to pull from and then encourage these students to speak out by giving a short opinion. After a few responses, you will see your shy students begin to feel comfortable responding in a supportive online environment.

Remember that, if you require all of your students to participate, the list of raised hands may be long. If students are impatient, they may assume they have been skipped over and may click the *enter* button before you call on them. Gently remind students to avoid speaking out of turn, and encourage them to be patient and orderly. If a particular student speaks out of turn repeatedly or is rude or overly critical, then a brief email reminding the student of online etiquette rules, including your policy on respecting others, usually solves the problem. If you find that there is general impatience and frustration resulting from a long list of participants, you could limit the number of responders per topic or discussion question.

The key to live chat is to engage your participants by keeping the discussion both active and moving forward. Since the success of live chat depends primarily on student involvement and secondarily on live lecture, prepare a list of discussion questions, and keep these handy. Always prepare more than you need just in case. Then, simply check each completed item off your list. Remember that you control the tempo and topic. The more backup items that you bring to the table, the more at ease and in control you will feel. What is most crucial to your success? You will feel confident conducting a live chat session if your etiquette rules are clear, if you take charge and call on your students as they raise their hands, and if you encourage them, through your own example, to show respect to all participants.

One of the most effective aspects of real-time discussion is the ability to have instantaneous communication. Many students thrive in this invigorating environment, and so will you! If you choose not to include live chat or you are not offered a synchronous course, you still have the option to incorporate a live element into your classroom by maintaining a live virtual office hour. You will come to find that your students will feel more connected and bonded to you if they can speak with you live—they will feel as if they are actually with you in your office.

Small-Group Chat Rooms

In the synchronous online class, small-group chat rooms can be one of the most integral and engaging portions of an online course, and they will make your whole-class chats that much more engaging. Small-group chat rooms provide excellent avenues for students to bond with one another as this venue offers a multitude of opportunities to discuss course material in more depth. This group activity is very conducive, if not necessary, to ensure successful live group presentations, should you include them in your curriculum. Assigning five to six students per small group seems to be an effective number for productive discourse. One of these group members can then be selected to moderate a group presentation in your whole-class chat room. As with all group activities, choose your participants wisely! Avoid placing all of the vocal, high-profile students together in one group. When sorting groups in the LMS, make sure that you include yourself as a member of each group so you can participate in each group chat room when necessary.

Taking attendance and monitoring participation in small groups is relatively simple as long as your LMS system allows you to automatically record and store chat sessions (most LMSs allow for this feature). If small-group chat follows a whole-class discussion forum, then the attendance is usually pretty solid. Most students really enjoy the experience and intimacy of small groups, and we've often found that the students conduct themselves in lively and intelligent manners. With such a small number of participants, many of your more rigorous etiquette rules, such as mandating your students to raise their hands, will not apply. Many have commented to us that small-group chat is one of their favorite aspects of our courses (and much less stressful than whole-class chat), for they appreciate the opportunity to express more in-depth thoughts on the course material.

We set permanent small groups (more preferable to us than fluid groups) at the beginning of the semester, usually after the third week when enrollment has settled. Set up groups as you would in a traditional classroom. Group members can be randomly selected, chosen alphabetically, chosen based on a mixture of compatibility and skill, or selected based on student preference. Although we ask our students if they would like to work with an individual or a group of individuals, we make sure the groups have a balance of vocal, confident, and competent students. One must consider attrition and the consequences of having a live chat presentation decimated by absent and absent-minded students!

Adding Variety: Mixing Chat and Forums

Your synchronous virtual classroom will most likely contain a mix of small-group and whole-class chat rooms along with small-group and whole-class discussion forums. It is vital that the meeting times and lengths for each component be made clear on your schedule and on the LMS course page. We suggest posting highly visible links to the chat rooms and forums next to the times of the activities.

When setting up your synchronous course, you'll want to consider how to best keep the students engaged during the lengthy three-hour meeting time. Real-time chat discussion works most effectively if it follows a whole-class forum discussion. Since forums are essentially teacher-free, they provide a safe exchange of ideas. So, beginning your weekly class with a whole-class forum discussion enhances live chat since students will have had the opportunity to bounce their ideas off one another. Forum discussions, when they precede chat, encourage student participation in the live chat room. Think of forum discussions as a warm-up exercise for chat discussions.

When discussion forums serve as part of a three-hour class block, we recommend requiring the students to post their initial responses early in order to maximize the effectiveness of live discussion time. Then, you can set aside the first hour of your class meeting for students to return to the forum to respond to their peers. Depending on the breadth of your forum prompt, you can also ask students to post their initial analyses and peer responses all within this first hour. As previously suggested in our asynchronous section above, you may require students to respond to responses made to their original post to increase the dialogue between the students—we recommend trying this approach at least once, so you can see how it increases the dialogue in your other live discussions, such as chat. After students have had the opportunity to read and respond to their peers' ideas, continue the discussion in live chat. Designate a firm cut-off time and lateness policy for forum posts, so students don't continue posting in the forum during your live chat session.

Maximize your students' attention and participation by scheduling a variety of short and long activities into your weekly agenda; after your one-hour discussion forum, designate a one-half to one-hour small-group chat, followed by a one-hour whole-class chat, or skip the small-group option and simply engage in a two-hour whole-class live chat discussion. Should you choose a longer chat session, be sure to schedule in a five- or ten-minute break here and there—it will do wonders to help you and your students keep focused on the conversation. Again, clearly indicate all meeting times and locations, so everyone will be in the designated place at the correct time.

Troubleshooting Technology

During the course of the semester, you will find that technical glitches can and will occur. The important thing to remember is to have a backup plan—at least one if not two. Inform your students ahead of time what to do if they cannot access your course material or, even worse, if the LMS system malfunctions. Here are a few troubleshooting tricks:

1. Require students to upload an alternate browser onto their desktops. Oftentimes, Internet Explorer or Safari malfunctions or is not consistently compatible with the LMS's learning components. Mozilla Firefox seems to be a safe option, but we do suggest having a backup browser already installed on all computers.

2. If students cannot access the LMS, a good starting point would be to suggest that they download the most recent versions of Java (from Sun Microsystems) and Adobe Flash. After downloading, instruct them to restart their computers.

3. Provide your students with your IT support webpage address, phone number, and contact information. Students may email you with a problem you cannot solve. Direct them to your IT department.

4. Keep apprised of scheduled LMS maintenance and the daily performance of your institution's web system. Campus-wide outages are usually reported via email to all faculty, and you can forward any pertinent information to your class.

5. Provide your students with a backup plan well in advance of any possible problem. Should the LMS be inaccessible during class time, send an instructional email to the class LISTSERV via your institution's email system. You won't be able to access the LMS email system if it is offline for repair.

6. If your campus website experiences a system-wide failure and crashes completely, no one will be able to access your course unless you use web features external to your institution's server. Do your best to contact your students, then revise your weekly activities and schedule accordingly.

Summary

As you embark on your online adventure, we recommend that you find several ways to display your course information for your students. LMSs offer a variety of features, and you will have the option to display your information either on your main course page or via forums, links, or email. Clarity and repetition are valuable attributes. Creating a reliable backup plan to disseminate your course schedule is also vital to the success of an online course should technical difficulties occur. Once you feel comfortable using the LMS, we recommend that you learn how to create and maintain a web presence via HTML and xHTML/CSS webpages. An email LISTSERV (whether created through the LMS or your institution) will also provide a key means of consistent communication.

Within your LMS, you'll find that whole-class forums will constitute a core component of your online course and will provide an effective environment for students to interact with the material and with one another. We have found that it's best, though, to keep the teacher's voice out of the forums as the students will then be more likely to participate in creative and empowered dialogues. If live chat is an option, we highly recommend implementing this engaging component into your curriculum. Students enjoy real-time dialogue and debate, and so will you!

LMS assessment tools provide an effective means for evaluating student performance. Grade book features allow for the option of automatic grade calculation, although we recommend manual grading for longer written essays, so you can check for originality and plagiarism. Some software programs provide pre-set comments that address style and grammar concerns; you may also create your own comment templates and store them in a document for future semesters. Incorporating quizzes into your curriculum adds inventive variety to the learning experience, and the automatic grading feature can save you precious time.

When working with technology, you'll find that glitches will occur; as long as you incorporate an effective backup plan into your course, you'll breeze through any temporary mishaps. Provide your students with valuable troubleshooting tricks, so they can be prepared for any problem. By following these guidelines, you'll discover you have all the material you need to create a dynamic and interactive online classroom!

5

Planning Future Semesters

Congratulations! You have successfully embarked on your journey into the venue of online education. You are now a card-carrying member of the Web 2.0 virtual learning environment. Take some time to savor the moment and pat yourself on the back as you pause and reflect on your accomplishments. As you review and evaluate your experiences, know that planning and implementing online course activities becomes easier. In this chapter, we offer a few suggestions to assist you in evaluating your current course and in constructing future courses.

Prior to the close of your teaching semester, we highly recommend that you create a course assessment forum wherein you ask students to rate course activities and evaluate your chosen learning modules. In order to maximize feedback, require students to post in this forum; if you make posting in this forum voluntary, you will likely receive few responses as students will be facing end-of-the-semester overload. As you create your semester-end evaluation forum, you may wish to construct a point system: Rate on a scale from 1 to 5 each activity's effectiveness. If you combine this with short-answer questions, you will receive comprehensive feedback. We suggest asking students to rate the course—not your performance. Objective review will be achieved most effectively by allowing some time to elapse before perusing the comments. Retain an open-minded perspective, and your future semesters will be greatly enhanced. We have included a list of suggested forum questions at the end of this chapter.

In our Preface, we suggested keeping a journal to record your semester's experiences. At the close of the semester, allow yourself a few weeks to relax, and then peruse your journal to determine which course activities created a dynamic and successful learning environment. Consider which learning modules or class time activities need changing or eliminating. Before ascertaining a course of action, compare your findings with the recommendations in the student survey.

As you analyze your course workload, evaluate the distribution of class activities. Take into consideration how much time you and your students need to prepare for class. Ask yourself, "How can I manage my time more effectively? How can I dispense the course requirements in a more efficient manner? How can I better engage my students in the subject matter?" To assist you in revisioning the structure and content of your course, we have included a semester-end checklist at the end of this chapter. In addition to time management, you will find questions pertaining to course format, discussion quality, student communication, and basic course redesign.

Additionally, we highly recommend a productive use of your semester break by attending workshops to assist you in learning new technologies. If you have yet to establish a web presence, attend a workshop on writing HTML code and webpage design. Perhaps you want to expand your use of the grade book, quiz, or media features. Inquire as to the availability of in-person training for specific features within your LMS. If on-campus workshops are not an option, explore the variety of training manuals provided by your institution.

As you keep abreast of the changes in the mainstream Internet, you will be better equipped to integrate new technologies into your virtual learning environment. Experiment with Facebook and Google to better understand trends in social networking. If you can understand the mind-set of the Web 2.0 learner, you will come to understand how they communicate through technology, and subsequently, you can best alter your curriculum to better meet their needs.

With consistent practice, your confidence will grow exponentially. During the early stages of your online teaching career, you will have an "aha!" moment when your new understanding of technology finally coalesces. This epiphany will lead to a cathartic breakthrough, and you will realize how much you are capable of accomplishing—you will come to embrace technology and want to expand your horizons to include more diverse avenues of communication and learning. Although there will always be challenges, you will succeed as long as you keep moving forward.

Your success in online education is limitless when you attain confidence in your methods. This confidence translates into an increased liveliness in the classroom, resulting in more fruitful and creative dialogues. Your future students will sense your ease working with the variant technologies, and sensing your ease will encourage them to engage more freely in academic discourse. The online classroom has the capability of assisting you in forging new pathways in the ever-growing, ever-changing Web 2.0 learning world!

Student Assessment Forum Questions

We have listed below a variety of assessment questions pertaining to online activities, time management, peer-to-peer interaction, and Internet etiquette. You needn't include all of these in one student assessment forum—simply choose what is appropriate for your needs.

- Were the course requirements and activities clearly outlined? Suggest ways for improvement.
- On a scale of 1 to 5 (5 being the highest), please rate our course activities:
  - Forum Discussion
  - Live Chat (if applicable)
  - Quizzes and Exams
  - Multimedia
  - Email LISTSERV
  - Small-Group Work (including group workshops, projects, and presentations)
  - Streaming Audio and Video (for lectures)
- Rate how you feel about the number of discussion forums: too many, too few, or just right.
- Rate the content of the forums and the depth of discussion.
- For those using live chat, how do you feel about the length and effectiveness of live chat? Would you like to see more or fewer small-group and whole-class chat sessions?
- In regard to live classes, were you able to accomplish forum posts in a satisfactory manner? In addition to the time allotted for chat, was there a sufficient amount of time for forum responses and other activities?
- How would you rate the effectiveness of peer-to-peer discussion? Did you learn about the course material by reading your peers' opinions? (If applicable, rate the effectiveness of group presentations).
- In general, did you find your peers to be open-minded when stating their opinions and listening to yours? If not, please suggest ways to improve the discussion.
- Did you find your peers to be respectful? If not, do you have any suggestions to improve the online etiquette rules?
- In regard to instructor involvement, was there too little, too much, or just the right amount? If you think there was too little, how would you like to see the instructor more involved in the online experience? If you think there was too much, at what points would you recommend the instructor be less involved?
- Please report any technical difficulties you experienced with the LMS or external links provided. Please note whether you have a Mac or a PC.

- What were your most enjoyable and least favorite activities? Were your most enjoyable activities also the best learning experiences? Were your least favorite activities also the worst learning experiences?
- Do you have any suggestions for additional technologies or resources for the online classroom?

End-of-Semester Checklist

At the close of the semester, spend some time reflecting on the success of your online course. Review the journal entries you made during the semester, and consider the feedback from your student assessment forum. Here are some questions to ponder:

- How can I manage my time more efficiently?
    - Do I spend too much time grading papers?
    - Can I reuse and then transfer more of my traditional course work into my online classroom?
    - What technical training will help me improve time management?

- How can I arrange course activities more effectively?
    - Am I using the calendar feature effectively to chronologically outline my course schedule?
    - For live classes, do I make meeting times and places clear?
    - Am I using the calendar to display embedded multimedia players?
    - Were my links to forums, quizzes, chats, assignments, lectures, external websites, and multimedia clearly displayed?
    - Do I provide a backup schedule on a course webpage?

- Evaluate the efficacy of my discussions:
    - How can I improve on the quality of discussion?
    - How can I increase meaningful participation?
    - If applicable, were my group projects, presentations, or workshops effective and efficient?

- How can I better communicate with my students?
    - Was the course email LISTSERV used adequately?
    - Was I able to clearly explain course requirements?
    - Are my comments visible and accessible to students?
    - Did I make my grades and grading policy clear and accessible?

- What learning modules would I like to add to future courses?
- How can I create a greater web presence at my institution?
- What in-person workshops can I attend?
- What how-to books should I read?
- What online tutorials and help forums should I take advantage of?

Appendix I

Sample Asynchronous Course Syllabus and Schedule

Humanities 101OL—The Forms & Ideas—Course Syllabus

Contact Information

Professor _____   Phone _____

Office Location _____   Email _____

Office Hours _____

Course Prerequisites

(Insert information from your institution's catalog.)

Enrollment Procedures (Note: the info below follows our university's procedures.)

Regularly enrolled students register for online courses in the same manner as they register for any course. If you wish to add the course after the semester begins, you must email the course professor for a permission number.

Students must email the instructor and receive an acknowledgement to complete the enrollment procedure. Directions will be given by the instructor about how to access the course website and complete the specific enrollment requirements.

Required Materials

1. *The Art of Being Human,* 9th Edition by Janaro and Altshuler

2. *Siddhartha* by Hermann Hesse

3. *Tao Te Ching* translated by Stephen Mitchell

4. *The Lord of the Rings: The Fellowship of the Ring*—2001 Peter Jackson Film

5. *What the Bleep Do We Know!?*—2004 Film

Student Learning Objectives

(Insert SLOs per your program's requirements.)

Course Requirements

Welcome to Humanities 101OL! This is an active-participation course that explores the various forms of human expression and thinking. During the semester, we will explore the worlds of art, music, philosophy, poetry, literature, morality, religion, and mythology. You will learn to successfully navigate the Internet and to engage in Moodle's asynchronous (bulletin board) forum discussions online.

Since this is mostly a discussion class, the success of this course depends on active participation. We will apply Reader Response Theory to all discussions. In other words, I want to hear how you, the reader, interact with the readings. All thoughtful opinions and insights are valued and welcomed— just be prepared to explain your theories!

During the course of the semester, you will be required to post written responses in whole-class Moodle forums and to post several major assignments on Turnitin. All responses are designed to reinforce the ideas presented in our course, enabling you to have a better understanding of the material.

Technical Requirements

Students will need to have access to the Internet—either Microsoft Internet Explorer, Firefox, Google Chrome, or Safari—and an active campus email account to access the Moodle system. To activate your campus email address or reset its password, use the *account utility page.*

Instructions will be provided for all computer activities; you may visit our *IT for Students* site for information on technical requirements and applications. Our campus also provides information on computer resources and availability. Please be familiar with our online applications, particularly Moodle, prior to our first meeting.

Note: For chat preparation, install Java before using chat! Because of a legal dispute between Microsoft and Sun, recent versions of Internet Explorer and Windows do not come bundled with Java, a program that Moodle chat relies on. If you try to use a Java-based program and Java has not been installed on your system, you will see a message indicating that you need to download Java Virtual Machine. You may download and install Java directly from Sun at http://www.java.com/en/index.jsp (click the big, yellow *Get It Now* button on that page). Follow the directions for installation, closing your web browser and restarting your system as it suggests. Once Java has been installed, you should encounter no further trouble with Moodle chat.

Accessibility

(Place your institution's accessibility statement here.)

Course Policies

Grading

Your final grade will be determined as follows:

1. Response to Text Readings: 35%
2. Art Analysis Paper: 20%
3. *Lord of the Rings* Film Analysis: 15%
4. *Siddhartha* Analysis: 15%
5. *What the Bleep Do We Know?!* Film Analysis: 15%

Attendance and Late Work

Please post your responses by the due dates in our schedule. Since this online class is time arranged, you may post your work early, but remember to revisit the whole-class forums to read and respond to your peers. Please note that late posts will be marked down one full grade per week. You will not receive credit for assignments posted more than ____ weeks late.

Carefully read each homework assignment. For text assignments, you will be required to respond in whole-class Moodle forums. For our major assignments (Art Paper, *LOTR, Siddhartha, Bleep*), you will be asked to post in a forum and post a major paper on Turnitin.

Whole-class forum postings will be graded 'A' for effort and thoughtfulness. Please leave yourself enough time to read and respond to your peers. You will receive a letter grade for each assignment posted on Turnitin.

Note that each whole-class forum has its own question and posting instructions—please click on the threaded discussion link listed on our Moodle page. Should you have any questions, please do not hesitate to email me.

Academic Dishonesty

(Place your institution's policy here.)

Course Links

- Syllabus
- Schedule
- Internet Etiquette in Our Discussion Forums
- Student Conduct Code
- Moodle
- Humanities Program

Links to Lectures and Readings

- Art of Being Human
- Critical Thinker
- How to Analyze Art
- Art Discussion Outline
- Extended Art Notes
- Online Art Gallery
- Mythology Discussion
- Fables and Fairytales
- Hero Myth Outline
- *LOTR* Discussion
- How to Analyze Poetry
- Elements of Fiction
- Literary Theory
- "The Story of an Hour"
- Religion Discussion

- Happiness Discussion
- *Siddhartha* Discussion
- Morality Discussion
- Love Discussion
- *Bleep* Discussion

Links to Major Assignments (Post on Turnitin!)

- Art Museum Paper
- *LOTR* Film Analysis
- *Siddhartha* Analysis
- *What the Bleep Do We Know?!* Analysis

Humanities 101OL: The Forms & Ideas—Course Schedule

Week One: January 23rd–January 29th

Topic: The Art of Being Human

Please complete the following prior to the end of Week One:

- Email Instructor to Complete Registration.
- Review Technical Requirements on Course Syllabus.
- Review Plagiarism Statement and Student Conduct Code as listed on Course Syllabus.
- Read the chapter "The Humanities: Still Vital."
- Attend Course Lecture: The Art of Being Human.
- Participate in the Moodle Whole–Class Discussion Forum: The Art of Being Human.

A Note About Homework Assignments:

All homework assignments are listed under each week's subheading. Note: You are required to post both an initial analysis and responses to five (5) peers in each Moodle whole-class threaded discussion forum. Each week, initial forum analyses need to be posted by midnight Thursday. You will have all day Friday and Saturday to revisit the forum(s) to read and respond to peers. Make sure you have all of your work completed by the end of each week.

Week Two: January 30th–February 5th

Topic: You and the Humanities

Please complete the following prior to the end of Week Two:

- Read the chapter "Profile of the Critical Thinker."
- Review the lecture Critical Thinker.
- Participate in the Moodle Whole-Class Discussion Forum: Apollonian Versus Dionysian Personality Traits.
- Participate in the Moodle Whole-Class Discussion Forum: You and the Humanities.

Week Three: February 6th–February 12th

Topic: Fine Art

(Note: There are five (5) written requirements for our Art Chapter—the major Art Museum Visit paper to be posted on our Turnitin course page and four (4) whole-class discussion forums spread out over the next two weeks.)

Please complete the following prior to the end of Week Three:

- Read the handout How to Analyze Fine Art.
- Read the first half of the chapter on "Art" from the beginning of the chapter through the Impressionism section.
- Read our lectures: Art Discussion Outline and Extended Art Notes.
- Visit our Online Art Gallery. This PowerPoint presentation will enhance your understanding of the various genres of art.
- Participate in the Moodle Whole-Class Discussion Forum: Art Analysis—Part One.
- Participate in the Moodle Whole-Class Discussion Forum: Art Analysis—Part Two.
- Review the Art Paper assignment. The Art Paper needs to be posted on our Turnitin course page by midnight on Saturday of Week Five.

Week Four: February 13th–February 19th

Topic: Fine Art

Please complete the following prior to the end of Week Four:

- Read the second half of the chapter on "Art."
- Participate in the Moodle Whole-Class Discussion Forum: Art Analysis—Part Three.
- Participate in the Moodle Whole-Class Discussion Forum: Art Analysis—Part Four.
- Review the Art Paper assignment. The Art Paper needs to be posted on our Turnitin course page by midnight on Saturday of Week Five.

Week Five: February 20th–February 26th

Topic: Fine Art

Please complete the following prior to the end of Week Five:

- Post your Art Paper on our Turnitin course page by midnight Saturday.

Week Six: February 27th–March 5th

Topic: Mythology

Please complete the following prior to the end of Week Six:

- Read the chapter "Myth and the Origin of the Humanities."
- Read Myth Discussion Guide, Fables and Fairytales Handout, and Hero Myth Outline.

- Participate in the Moodle Whole-Class Discussion Forum: Myth Analysis— Part One.
- Participate in the Moodle Whole-Class Discussion Forum: Myth Analysis— Part Two.

Week Seven: March 6th–March 12th

Topic: Literature

Please complete the following prior to the end of Week Seven:

- Read the chapter on "Literature."
- Read How to Analyze Poetry, Fiction Analysis Handout, and Literary Theory.
- Read the short story: "The Story of an Hour."
- Participate in the Moodle Whole-Class Discussion Forum: Poetry Analysis.
- Participate in the Moodle Whole-Class Discussion Forum: "Story of an Hour" Analysis.
- View the 2001 film version of *Lord of the Rings: The Fellowship of the Ring* by the beginning of Week Eight.

Week Eight: March 13th–March 19th

Topic: Mythology and The Lord of the Rings (LOTR)

(Note: There are two (2) written requirements for *LOTR*—the major paper to be posted on our Turnitin course page and one (1) whole-class discussion forum.)

Please complete the following prior to the end of Week Eight:

- View the 2001 film version of *Lord of the Rings: The Fellowship of the Ring.*
- Read our *LOTR* Discussion Guide.
- Participate in the Moodle Whole-Class Discussion Forum: *LOTR* Themes of Life.
- Post your *Lord of the Rings-The Fellowship of the Ring* Major Paper on our Turnitin course page.

Week Nine: March 20th–March 26th

Topic: Religion

Please complete the following prior to the end of Week Nine:

- Read the chapter on "Religion."
- Read our Religion Lecture.

- Participate in the Moodle Whole-Class Discussion Forum: Some Questions You Might Ask.
- Participate in the Moodle Whole-Class Discussion Forum: Viva La Vida. Watch the music video on our Moodle page. I have embedded a video player in Week Nine of our calendar.

Week Ten: March 27th–April 2nd

Topic: The Tao Te Ching

Please complete the following prior to the end of Week Ten:

- Read the *Tao Te Ching*, translation by Stephen Mitchell.
- Participate in the Moodle Whole-Class Discussion Forum: Politics, War, Peace, and the *Tao Te Ching*.
- Participate in the Moodle Whole-Class Discussion Forum: Meaningful Tao Verses.
- Begin reading our novel, *Siddhartha*.

Week Eleven: April 3rd–April 9th— Spring Break—No Class

Week Twelve: April 10th–April 16th

Topic: Morality

Please complete the following prior to the end of Week Twelve:

- Read the chapter on "Morality."
- Read our Morality Discussion Guide.
- Participate in the Moodle Whole-Class Discussion Forum: Socrates and Plato.
- Participate in the Moodle Whole-Class Discussion Forum: Ethical Dilemma.
- Finish reading our novel, *Siddhartha*.

Week Thirteen: April 17th–April 23rd

Topic: Siddhartha

(Note: There are two (2) written requirements for *Siddhartha*—the major paper to be posted on our Turnitin course page and one (1) whole-class discussion forum.)

Please complete the following prior to the end of Week Thirteen:

- Finish reading *Siddhartha*.
- Read our *Siddhartha* Discussion Guide.

- Participate in the Moodle Whole-Class Discussion Forum: *Siddhartha*— Themes of Life.
- Post your *Siddhartha* major paper on our Turnitin course page by midnight on Saturday.

Week Fourteen: April 24th–April 30th

Topic: Happiness

Please complete the following prior to the end of Week Fourteen:

- Read the chapter on "Happiness."
- Read our Happiness Discussion Guide.
- Participate in the Moodle Whole-Class Discussion Forum: Be Happy!
- Participate in the Moodle Whole-Class Discussion Forum: How to Change the World!
- Plan your *What the Bleep Do We Know!?* major assignment: Create Your Day. The major paper is due Week Sixteen!
- View the 2004 film, *What the Bleep Do We Know?!*, by the beginning of Week Sixteen. The film can be viewed online at the following site: http://www.mov iesfoundonline.com/what_the_bleep_do_we_know.php

Week Fifteen: May 1st–May 7th

Topic: Love

Please complete the following prior to the end of Week Fifteen:

- Read the chapter on "Love."
- Read our Love Discussion Guide.
- Participate in the Moodle Whole-Class Discussion Forum: What Is Love?
- Participate in the Moodle Whole-Class Discussion Forum: All You Need is Love. Watch the video clip of this song on our Moodle page. I have embedded a video player in Week Fifteen of our calendar.
- Plan your *What the Bleep Do We Know!?* major assignment: Create Your Day. The major paper is due Week Sixteen!
- View the 2004 film *What the Bleep Do We Know?!*, by the beginning of Week Sixteen. The film can be viewed online at the following site: http://www.mov iesfoundonline.com/what_the_bleep_do_we_know.php

Week Sixteen: May 8th–May 14th

Topic: What the Bleep Do We Know?!

(Note: There are two (2) written requirements for *Bleep*—the major paper to be posted on our Turnitin course page and one (1) whole-class discussion forum.)

Please complete the following prior to the end of Week Sixteen:

- Read our *Bleepin'* Discussion Guide.
- Participate in the Moodle Whole-Class Discussion Forum: *What the Bleep?*
- Post your Create Your Day major paper on our Turnitin course page by midnight on Saturday!
- Post your comments in Our Assessment Forum.
- Have a wonderful summer!

Appendix II

Sample Synchronous Course Syllabus and Schedule

English 364OL—The Short Story—Course Syllabus

Contact Information

Professor _____ Phone _____

Office Location _____ Email _____

Office Hours _____

Course Prerequisites

(Insert information from your institution's catalog.)

Enrollment Procedures (Note: the info below follows our university's procedures.)

Regularly enrolled students register for online courses in the same manner as they register for any course. If you wish to add the course after the semester begins, you must email the course professor for a permission number.

Students must email the instructor and receive an acknowledgement to complete the enrollment procedure. Directions will be given by the instructor about how to access the course website and complete the specific enrollment requirements.

Required Materials

1. *Heath Introduction to Fiction,* 6th Edition by John J. Clayton, Editor

2. *Brokeback Mountain*—A Film by Ang Lee (rent or purchase)

3. *Brokeback Mountain Story to Screenplay*—Story by Annie Proulx, screenplay by Larry McMurtry and Diana Ossana

Student Learning Objectives

(Insert SLOs per your program's requirements.)

Course Requirements

Welcome to English 364OL, an upper division general education course in the genre of the short story! In this discussion-based virtual classroom, we will study a variety of stories with varying themes, written at different periods of time, and authored by a diverse group of writers. The goal of our course is to appreciate the short story as a genre of literature and to enhance students' analytical reading and writing skills.

Note: This class will meet live online every Wednesday from 7:00 p.m. to 9:45 p.m. Please check your availability before registering for this course. This is a live discussion-based course, so please plan to be online for the entire 2 3/4-hour class meeting!

Since this is mostly a discussion class, the success of this course depends on active participation. We will apply Reader Response Theory to all discussions. In other words, I want to hear how you, the reader, interact with the readings. All thoughtful opinions and insights are valued and welcomed—just be prepared to explain your theories! In addition, you will be required to work in permanent groups of four to six students throughout the semester. Part of our class time will be devoted to group activities and small-group chat rooms.

Technical Requirements

Students will need to have access to the Internet—either Microsoft Internet Explorer, Firefox, Google Chrome, or Safari—and an active campus email account to access the Moodle system. To activate your campus email address or reset its password, use the *account utility page.*

Instructions will be provided for all computer activities; you may visit our *IT for Students* site for information on technical requirements and applications. Our campus also provides information on computer resources and availability. Please be familiar with our online applications, particularly Moodle, prior to our first meeting.

Note: For chat preparation install Java before using chat! Because of a legal dispute between Microsoft and Sun, recent versions of Internet Explorer and Windows do not come bundled with Java, a program that Moodle chat relies on. If you try to use a Java-based program and Java has not been installed on your system, you will see a message indicating that you need to download Java Virtual Machine. You may download and install Java directly from Sun at http://www.java.com/en/index.jsp (click the big, yellow *Get It Now* button on that page). Follow the directions for installation, closing your web browser and restarting your system as it suggests. Once Java has been installed, you should encounter no further trouble with Moodle chat.

Accessibility

(Place your institution's accessibility statement here.)

Course Policies

Grading

Your final grade will be determined as follows:

1. Response to Anthology Readings: 60%

2. *Brokeback Mountain* Midterm Paper: 20%

3. Attendance, Preparation, Discussion, and Group Presentation: 20%

Note: In order to earn credit for participating in a chat, each student must make at least three (3) quality thoughtful comments per discussion. Fulfilling this mandatory requirement illustrates that you are satisfactorily interacting with the material.

Attendance and Late Work

Please come to our online discussions on time and prepared! Every absence will lower your overall grade. Should you miss more than three weeks of class (excused or unexcused), you will not be allowed to pass the course. Late papers and forum posts will be marked down one full grade per week and will adversely affect your overall class grade.

Academic Dishonesty

(Place your institution's policy here.)

Course Links

- Syllabus
- Schedule
- Internet Etiquette in Our Discussion Forums
- Student Conduct Code
- Moodle
- Department of English

Links to Lectures

- Elements of Fiction
- Literary Theory
- Myth & Archetype: The Hero's Quest
- Experimental Literature: Metafiction and Surrealism

Links to Major Assignments

- *Brokeback Mountain* Midterm Paper
- Group Story Presentation

English 364OL: The Short Story—Course Schedule

Week One: Wednesday, August 27th

Introduction to Course

Note: Please read and study the following links prior to our first class:

Email Instructor to Complete Registration.

Review Netiquette Rules: Internet Etiquette in Our Discussion Forums.

Read Technical Requirements for Moodle as listed on Course Syllabus.

Review the Plagiarism Statement and Student Conduct Code as listed on the Course Syllabus.

*Today's Schedule of Class Time Activities:

7:00 p.m.—Class Meets in Our Moodle Whole-Class Chat Room.

8:30 p.m.—Class Meets in Moodle Discussion Forum: Student Introductions.

Homework: Due 9/3

1. Practice Moodle Chat and Threaded Discussions! Click on our course links to visit the appropriate tutorials. You will need to be familiar and comfortable with the online applications by next week.

2. Reading Assignment Part One: Read "Introduction: On Fiction" pgs. 1–35. Take particular note of these aspects of literary analysis: POV—Point of View; Characterization; Dramatic Structure (emphasis on conflict); Imagery and Symbolism; Setting, Tone, and Voice; and Theme.

3. Reading Assignment Part Two: Read the following short stories:
   • "Everyday Use"
   • "The Lottery"

4. Writing Assignment: Post a response to "Everyday Use" and "The Lottery" in our Moodle Discussion Forum: Conflicts in Society prior to our next class meeting. You will have an opportunity to respond to your peers during next week's class time.

5. Course Lecture: Review the following online lecture: Elements of Fiction.

6. Special Note: All Moodle whole-class discussion forum postings will be graded 'A' for effort and thoughtfulness and will be calculated into your

overall participation grade. Initial responses must be posted prior to class time in order to be eligible to receive maximum credit. Please be on time to all live discussions, so you may have sufficient time to read and respond to your peers.

Carefully read each homework requirement—our week-to-week schedule will vary. For some stories, you will be required to post a response on Turnitin and post in a Whole-Class Forum. On occasion, you will be required to respond in only one way—a forum or Turnitin. For Turnitin responses, you will be asked to analyze specific elements that are listed in the homework requirements.

For Whole-Class Forums, you will find that each Moodle forum has its own question and posting instructions. You will need to post your responses to all our readings before the class meetings. You will not earn credit for posts made during scheduled chat times. Consider our Whole-Class Forums as part of our class discussion.

Throughout the semester, we will discuss our ideas in two formats: Whole-Class Moodle Forums and Live Chat Rooms. Each environment offers advantages for a thorough discussion and exchange of ideas. Whole-Class Forums are "teacher-free" and offer you the opportunity to "hear" from every student in class and enjoy reading and responding to a variety of perspectives and points of view!

Week Two: Wednesday, September 3rd

Literary Theme: Conflicts in Society

Discuss "The Lottery" and "Everyday Use."

*Today's Schedule of Class Time Activities:

7:00 p.m.—Class Meets in Our Moodle Discussion Forum: Conflicts in Society.

8:00 p.m.—Class Meets in Our Moodle Whole-Class Chat Room.

Homework: Due 9/10

1. Course Lecture: Review the following online lecture: Literary Theory.

2. Reading Assignment Part One: Read "How to Read and Write About Fiction" pgs. 37–49.

3. Surf the Internet for sites on Civil Rights and the Civil Rights Movement. Be prepared to share your URLs and general site information with the class in our Moodle Whole-Class Discussion Forum.

4. Reading Assignment Part Two: Read the following short stories:
   - "Sonny's Blues"
   - "A Worn Path"

5. Writing Assignment Part One: Post a response to both stories on Turnitin prior to our next class meeting. Write a 250-word analysis for each, analyzing each story's use of narration. Discuss any evidence of "unreliable" narration or character bias—from the first-person or third-person point of view. You will receive a letter grade for each story analysis.

6. Writing Assignment Part Two: Post your Civil Rights Internet URLs in our Moodle Discussion Forum: Oppression and Civil Rights prior to our next class meeting. You will have an opportunity to respond to your peers during next week's class time.

Week Three: Wednesday, September 10th

Literary Theme: Conflicts of Oppression and Narrator Bias or Point of View

Discuss "Sonny's Blues" and "A Worn Path."

Discuss Literary Theory.

*Today's Schedule of Class Time Activities:

7:00 p.m.—Class Meets in Our Moodle Discussion Forum: Oppression and Civil Rights.

7:45 p.m.—Class Meets in Our Moodle Whole-Class Chat Room.

Homework: Due 9/17

1. Reading Assignment: Read the following short stories:
   - "Hills Like White Elephants"
   - "Cathedral"

2. Writing Assignment: Post a response to "Hills Like White Elephants" and "Cathedral" in our Moodle Discussion Forum: Minimalist Style prior to our next class meeting. You will have an opportunity to respond to your peers during next week's class time.

Week Four: Wednesday, September 17th

Literary Theme: Minimalism, Subtext, and Relationships

Discuss "Hills Like White Elephants" and "Cathedral."

*Today's Schedule of Class Time Activities:

7:00 p.m.—Class Meets in Our Moodle Discussion Forum: Minimalist Style.

7:45 p.m.—Groups Meet in Small-Group Live Chat Rooms.

Exchange email addresses, phone numbers, and so on, and spend this time getting to know each other!

- Blue Group: TBA
- Red Group: TBA
- Green Group: TBA
- Teal Group: TBA
- Purple Group: TBA
- Orange Group: TBA

8:15 p.m.—Class Meets in Our Moodle Whole-Class Chat Room

Homework: Due 9/24

1. Reading Assignment: Read the following short stories:
   - "The Rocking-Horse Winner"
   - "Araby"

2. Course Lecture: Review the following online lecture: Myth and Archetype: The Hero's Quest.

3. Writing Assignment Part One: Like so many stories in our anthology, "The Rocking-Horse Winner" is shaped by initiation—perhaps even a dark initiation. Discuss the boy's "initiation" into adulthood (and subsequent conflicts) as you post a 250-word analysis of the Lawrence story on Turnitin prior to next week's class time. Note that the main character follows both the hero archetype and the Oedipus Complex Theory in mythology; you may wish to compare the boy's "ordinary" world to his "special" world and/or initiation into adulthood.

4. Writing Assignment Part Two: Post a response to "Araby" in our Moodle Discussion Forum: Araby prior to our next class meeting. You will have an opportunity to respond to your peers during next week's class time.

Week Five: Wednesday, September 24th

Literary Theme: Setting, Identity, and The Hero's Journey

Discuss "The Rocking-Horse Winner" and "Araby."

*Today's Schedule of Class Time Activities:

7:00 p.m.—Class Meets in Our Moodle Discussion Forum: Araby.

7:45 p.m.—Groups Meet in Small-Group Live Chat Rooms.

Discuss the characters' search for personal identity (conflicts and themes of initiation and/or growth) and the use of symbolic language and images.

8:15 p.m.—Class Meets in Our Moodle Whole-Class Chat Room.

Homework: Due 10/1

1. Surf the Internet for sites on the Women's Suffrage Movement. Be prepared to share your URLs and ideas on women's roles throughout history, particularly the time periods of this week's assigned stories, with the class in our Whole-Class Discussion Forum.

2. Reading Assignment: Read the following short stories:
   • "The Yellow Wall-Paper"
   • "I Stand Here Ironing"

3. Writing Assignment Part One: Post a 250-word analysis of each story on Turnitin prior to next week's class time. Emphasize the characters and their conflicts (treatment of women in society) according to Feminist & Historicist Literary Theory.

4. Writing Assignment Part Two: In addition, post your Women's Suffrage Movement Internet URLs in our Moodle Discussion Forum: Conflicts of Women prior to our next class meeting. You will have an opportunity to respond to your peers during next week's class time.

Week Six: Wednesday, October 1st

Literary Theme: Conflicts of Women

Discuss "The Yellow Wall-Paper" and "I Stand Here Ironing."

*Today's Schedule of Class Time Activities:

7:00 p.m.—Class Meets in Our Moodle Discussion Forum: Conflicts of Women.

7:30 p.m.—Groups Meet in Small-Group Live Chat Rooms.

Discuss the meaning of each story's title and examine each story from a Feminist and Historicist POV as you discuss the role of women in 19th- and 20th-Century America.

8:00 p.m.—Class Meets in Our Moodle Whole-Class Chat Room.

Homework: Due 10/8

1. Reading Assignment: Read the following short stories:
   - "The Man I Killed"
   - "The Lives of the Dead"

2. Writing Assignment: Post a response to the Tim O'Brien stories in our Moodle Discussion Forum: O'Brien Stories prior to our next class meeting. You will have an opportunity to respond to your peers during next week's class time.

3. Midterm Assignment—Due in Two Weeks—October 15th: For your midterm paper, you are required to read *Brokeback Mountain, Story to Screenplay* and view the 2005 Ang Lee film *Brokeback Mountain*. The assignment is posted online: *Brokeback Mountain* Midterm Paper Assignment. Post your analysis on Turnitin prior to midnight on Wednesday, October 15th. In order to give you sufficient time to prepare and complete the midterm, we will not meet as a class on October 15th.

Week Seven: Wednesday, October 8th

Literary Theme: The Trauma of War

Discuss "The Man I Killed" and "The Lives of the Dead."

*Today's Schedule of Class Time Activities:

7:00 p.m.—Class Meets in Our Moodle Discussion Forum: O'Brien Stories.

7:45 p.m.—Class Meets in Our Moodle Whole-Class Chat Room.

Homework: Due 10/15

1. Midterm Assignment—Due Next Week: For your midterm paper, you are required to read *Brokeback Mountain, Story to Screenplay* and view the

2005 Ang Lee film *Brokeback Mountain*. The assignment is posted online: *Brokeback Mountain* Midterm Paper Assignment. Post your analysis on Turnitin prior to midnight on Wednesday, October 15th. In order to give you sufficient time to prepare and complete the midterm, we will not meet as a class next week. Good luck and enjoy this story-to-screenplay analysis experience!

Week Eight: Wednesday, October 15th

Midterm Week! No Live Chat!

Post your midterm paper on Turnitin prior to midnight!

Homework: Due 10/22

1. Group Presentation: Read the Group Short Story Presentation Assignment. You will have time in our next class to meet in your small-group chat rooms to discuss possible story selections. Scan through the unassigned stories in our text, and select several choices to discuss with your group. Only one group can present a given story—so discuss several options. Note: Only consider stories that have not been assigned—check the entire schedule!

Week Nine: Wednesday, October 22nd

Brokeback Mountain Discussion

Groups Select a Story for Presentation.

*Today's Schedule of Class Time Activities:

7:00 p.m.—Class Meets in Our Moodle Whole-Class Chat Room.

Homework: Due 10/29

1. Reading Assignment: Read the following short stories:
   - "The Magic Barrel"
   - "Idiots First"
2. Writing Assignment: Post a response in our Moodle Discussion Forum: Malamud's Moral Compassion prior to our next class meeting. You will have an opportunity to respond to your peers during next week's class time.

Week Ten: Wednesday, October 29th

Literary Theme: Moral Compassion

Discuss "The Magic Barrel" and "Idiots First."

*Today's Schedule of Class Time Activities:

7:00 p.m.—Class Meets in Our Moodle Discussion Forum: Malamud's Moral Compassion.

7:45 p.m.—Class Meets in Our Moodle Whole-Class Chat Room.

9:00 p.m.—Groups Meet in Small-Group Live Chat Rooms to work on story presentations!

Homework: Due 11/5

1. Reading Assignment: Read the following short stories:
   - "The Jilting of Granny Weatherall"
   - "A Rose for Emily"

2. Writing Assignment: Post a response to both stories on Turnitin prior to our next class meeting. Write a 250-word analysis for each, applying Psychological Literary Theory to the main female characters (Granny and Emily). In other words, psychoanalyze any actions, emotions, ideas, relationships, and so on, in order to determine each character's psychological state of mind. You may discuss pertinent symbols, character personality traits, and conflicts to support your ideas.

3. Group Presentations: Continue work on group presentations.

Week Eleven: Wednesday, November 5th

Literary Theme: Psychological Literary Theory

Discuss "The Jilting of Granny Weatherall" and "A Rose for Emily."

*Today's Schedule of Class Time Activities:

7:00 p.m.—Class Meets in Our Moodle Whole-Class Chat Room.

8:30 p.m.—Groups Meet in Small-Group Live Chat Rooms to work on story presentations!

Homework: Due 11/12

1. Reading Assignment: Read the following short stories:
   - "A Very Old Man With Enormous Wings"
   - "A Hunger Artist"

2. Course Lecture: Review the following online lecture: Experimental Literature: Metafiction and Surrealism.

3. Writing Assignment: Post a response to both stories in our Moodle Discussion Forum: Fantasy and Magical Realism prior to our next class meeting. You will have an opportunity to respond to your peers during next week's class time.

4. Group Presentations: Continue work on group presentations.

Week Twelve: Wednesday, November 12th

Literary Theme: Fantasy and Magical Realism

Discuss "A Very Old Man With Enormous Wings" and "A Hunger Artist."

*Today's Schedule of Class Time Activities:

- 7:00 p.m.—Class Meets in Our Moodle Discussion Forum: Fantasy and Magical Realism.
- 7:45 p.m.—Class Meets in Our Moodle Whole-Class Chat Room.
- 9:00 p.m.—Groups Meet in Small-Group Live Chat Rooms to work on story presentations!

Homework: Due 11/19

1. Read the following short stories:
   - "My Life With the Wave"
   - "How I Finally Lost My Heart"

2. Writing Assignment: Post a response to both stories in our Moodle Discussion Forum: Experimental Literature prior to our next class meeting. You will have an opportunity to respond to your peers during next week's class time.

3. Group Presentations: Continue work on group presentations. Presentations for Red, Teal, and Purple Groups Due 12/3! Presentations for Blue, Green, and Orange Groups Due 12/10! Read all stories prior to presentations!
   - Blue Group Story: "The Bucket Rider" by Franz Kafka
   - Red Group Story: "The Lady with the Dog" by Anton Chekhov

- Green Group Story: "Lust" by Susan Minot
- Teal Group Story: "The Fall of the House of Usher" by Edgar Allan Poe
- Purple Group Story: "The Man Who Could See Radiance" by John J. Clayton
- Orange Group Story: "Hansel and Gretel" by Jacob and Wilhelm Grimm

4. Groups post Story Presentations in Moodle group presentation forums on the weekend prior to their scheduled presentation!

5. Reminder: Post your responses in each group's Moodle discussion forum prior to the group's scheduled whole-class chat room presentation and discussion!

Week Thirteen: Wednesday, November 19th

Literary Theme: Experimental Techniques

Discuss "My Life With the Wave" and "How I Finally Lost My Heart."

*Today's Schedule of Class Time Activities:

7:00 p.m.—Class Meets in Our Moodle Discussion Forum: Experimental Literature.

7:45 p.m.—Class Meets in Our Moodle Whole-Class Chat Room.

9:00 p.m.—Groups Meet in Small-Group Live Chat Rooms to work on story presentations!

Homework: Due 11/26

1. Group Presentations: Continue work on group presentations. Groups arrange to meet next week to finalize presentations. I am available to join you in your small-group chat rooms by appointment only.

2. Presentations for Red, Teal, and Purple Groups Due 12/3! Presentations for Blue, Green, and Orange Groups Due 12/10! Read all stories prior to presentations!

3. Groups post Story Presentations in Moodle group presentation forums on the weekend prior to the scheduled presentation!

4. Reminder: Post your responses in each group's Moodle discussion forum prior to the group's scheduled whole-class chat room presentation and discussion!

Week Fourteen: Wednesday, November 26th

No Live Whole-Class Chat!

Groups Arrange to Meet in Small-Group Chat Rooms!

Homework: Due 12/3

1. Group Presentations: Finalize work on group presentations. Presentations for Red, Teal, and Purple Groups Due 12/3! Presentations for Blue, Green, and Orange Groups Due 12/10! Read all stories prior to presentations!

2. Groups post Story Presentations in Moodle group presentation forums on the weekend prior to the scheduled presentation!

3. Reminder: Post your responses in each group's Moodle discussion forum prior to the group's scheduled whole-class chat room presentation and discussion!

Week Fifteen: Wednesday, December 3rd

Red, Teal, and Purple Group Presentations!

*Today's Schedule of Class Time Activities:

Prior to Class Time Post All Responses to Moodle Group Presentation Forums!

7:00 p.m.—Class Meets in Our Moodle Whole-Class Chat Room.

Homework: Due 12/10

1. Group Presentations: Finalize work on group presentations. Presentations for Blue, Green, and Orange Groups due next week!

2. Groups post Story Presentations in Moodle group presentation forums on the weekend prior to the scheduled presentation!

3. Reminder: Post your responses in each group's Moodle discussion forum prior to the group's scheduled whole-class chat room presentation and discussion!

Week Sixteen: Wednesday, December 10th

Blue, Green, and Orange Group Presentations!

*Today's Schedule of Class Time Activities:

Prior to Class Time Post All Responses to Moodle Group Presentation Forums!

7:00 p.m.—Class Meets in Our Moodle Whole-Class Chat Room.

9:30 p.m.—Class Meets in Our Assessment Forum.

Appendix III
Internet Etiquette Guidelines

To practice respectful behavior and to avoid mass chaos (and migraines!) in our whole-class chat rooms and forums, please adhere to the following discussion guidelines:

- Be open-minded to all viewpoints.
- Do not speak out of turn. Please wait for the instructor to call on you.
- Avoid shouting. Typing in ALL CAPS IS SHOUTING!
- Avoid profanity.
- Speak kindly and respectfully to each other and the instructor.
- Practice patience.

To give a sense of order to the whole-class chat sessions, the following will apply:

- The instructor serves as chat room moderator.
- Avoid greeting your classmates as they enter the chat room.
- When you want to make a comment, type an "!" and wait until the instructor types your name. This is the equivalent of raising your hand.
- When you want to ask a question, type a "?" and wait until the instructor types your name.
- Please do not type an ! or a ? repeatedly. You will be called on in order, so be patient.
- When you are speaking, use the ellipses marks " . . ." to indicate that you are still typing and will be continuing your thought.
- When you are done speaking, use normal punctuation, or type "end."

If everyone follows the above etiquette rules, our class discussions will be productive, cohesive, and engaging.

Keep in mind that the same courtesies apply in our threaded forum discussions. Be supportive and kind; please report any student who engages in disrespectful and unprofessional behavior.

Thank you for your patience and understanding!

Index

About the Authors

Pat Swenson holds a Master of Fine Arts Degree in Creative Writing from Goddard College and a Master's Degree in English from California State University, Northridge (CSUN), where she currently teaches English and Humanities. During her 20-year tenure at CSUN, she has developed and maintained a comprehensive website providing online resources for K–12 educators. She also served as both webmaster for the Humanities Program and as faculty representative on the Educational Technology Committee. Her efforts on the Committee culminated in securing online course offerings in the English Department. The recipient of numerous educational grants, she coordinated and evaluated key pilot programs to advance the implementation of online curricula.

Nancy A. Taylor holds a Master's Degree in English Literature from California State University, Northridge (CSUN), where she currently teaches English and Humanities. For the past 15 years, she has taught traditional and online courses and has served on the English Department Educational Technology Committee. She has been awarded numerous educational grants related to the integration or improvement of online technology as it relates to learning and curriculum, including the development, implementation, and evaluation of pilot programs and expanding the functionality and applicability of educational websites. She has also served as a webmaster for the Humanities Program.

⑤SAGE research methods online

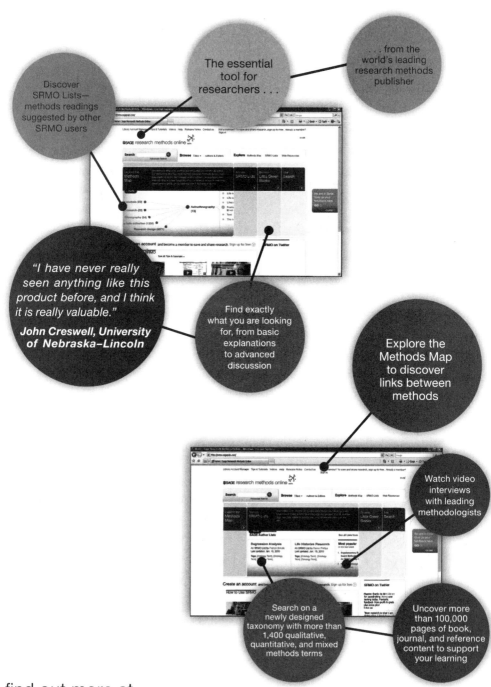

The essential tool for researchers . . .

. . . from the world's leading research methods publisher

Discover SRMO Lists— methods readings suggested by other SRMO users

"I have never really seen anything like this product before, and I think it is really valuable."
John Creswell, University of Nebraska–Lincoln

Find exactly what you are looking for, from basic explanations to advanced discussion

Explore the Methods Map to discover links between methods

Watch video interviews with leading methodologists

Search on a newly designed taxonomy with more than 1,400 qualitative, quantitative, and mixed methods terms

Uncover more than 100,000 pages of book, journal, and reference content to support your learning

find out more at
www.srmo.sagepub.com